CELEBRATING FAITH

CELEBRATING
Faith
Year-Round Activities for Catholic Families

MARY CRONK FARRELL

ST. ANTHONY MESSENGER PRESS
Cincinnati, Ohio

The song "Washerwoman God" reprinted with permission of the author.

Scripture passages have been taken from *New Revised Standard Version Bible*, copyright ©1989 by the Division of Christian Education of the National Council of the Churches of Christ in the U.S.A., and used by permission. All rights reserved.

Cover design by Mark Sullivan
Book design by Sandy L. Digman

Library of Congress Cataloging-in-Publication Data

Farrell, Mary Cronk.
  Celebrating faith: year-round activities for Catholic families/Mary Cronk Farrell.
      p. cm.
  ISBN 0-86716-661-4 (pbk. : alk. paper) 1. Family—Religious life. 2. Catholic Church—Customs and practices. 3. Church year. I. Title.

BX2351.F365 2005
249'.088'282-dc22

                                                            2005016203

ISBN 0-86716-661-4
Published by St. Anthony Messenger Press
28 W. Liberty St.
Cincinnati, OH 45202
www.AmericanCatholic.org

Printed in the United States of America

Printed on acid-free paper
05 06 07 08 09 5 4 3 2 1

To Lori and Robert Fontana,
with love and gratitude.

CONTENTS

Acknowledgments

So many people have been instrumental in the process that brought me to the writing of this book that it is impossible to thank them all. But I must mention a few. I'm indebted to Deacon Eric Meisfjord for giving me the opportunity to begin writing on the topic of family spirituality and for continuing to publish my columns in the Catholic Diocese of Spokane's *Inland Register* over the years. I'm grateful to all the loyal readers whose encouraging comments have kept me going.

I'm grateful to Therese Covert, Cheryl Doran and Jennifer Akins, whose friendship sustains me daily in my parenting efforts. I am also grateful to the *Fireside Chatters*, the Catholic Community of St. Ann, and my faithful writing groups. I'd be lost without you all.

To my family who loves me as I stumble and fall again and again, and who celebrates my success as well: thank you Mike, Brandon, Monica and Dylan. I love you.

Introduction

IF YOU ARE LOOKING AT THIS BOOK, you are most likely a parent who understands the importance of providing a spiritual dimension to family life. You want to give your children a solid foundation in the Christian faith. Perhaps you're just starting your family, or you are well into raising children and, despite your determination, you have discovered this is no easy task. You take your family to church on Sunday and you strive to teach them right from wrong during the week. But sometimes you run out of time and energy. Or you lack simple ways to communicate important concepts of faith to your kids. You may feel isolated in a culture that puts activities like sports before worship. You need support countering media messages that consumer goods are the way to happiness.

This book seeks to provide you with practical help in teaching your children Christian values and fostering faith in everyday family life. Each chapter offers ways to celebrate the church's liturgical year, as well as secular holidays. You will find simple explanations of the church seasons and major holy days. Scripture readings, simple prayers, rituals and activities are suggested throughout, as well as true stories from family life meant to inspire, encourage and offer food for thought.

As you use this book, be conscious of the needs and gifts of your own family. The ideas presented are meant as suggestions. They may be exactly right for you, or merely serve as starting points from which to develop your own traditions and practices. No family could do everything in this book. There is real danger in trying to do too much or in forcing preconceived formulas. My underlying purpose in this book is to support you in seeing and nurturing the holy that is already present in your home. All of family life is sacred. There is grace in the messiness and struggle as well as in the joy and success.

This is not a book you'll read once, but one you will want to keep handy and refer to often. Use *Celebrating Faith* as a companion in celebrating holidays. Flip through the pages of "Ordinary Time" for tips on teaching kids to pray, or check out "Autumn Ember Days" to discover how the power of story strengthens family bonds. I designed short sections to deliver quick information on busy days. You'll find the book helpful year after year as your children grow in maturity and faith.

1

THE NEW YEAR
Centering at Home

The New Year often brings a mix of emotions. This period of the old giving way to the new can be exciting as well as unsettling. Our culture celebrates with glitz and revelry, but the season can be a dark time for some families. Parents are often worn out after the holiday season. Children may feel let down when Christmas Day is over, and they often dread the routine of school after vacation. In climates where it is dark and cold, January can be gloomy.

Use these first months of the year as a time to center around home and relationships. Anchor your family with activities and rituals that foster a sense of togetherness, security and dependence on God. Take time to clear clutter from your life and focus on the riches of creativity, spirituality and friendship. A simpler life leaves us more time, more space and more energy. Your efforts in this direction will help form a firm ground in the face of changes bound to come in the New Year and allow for reaching beyond your family to the wider community.

The Feast of Epiphany, one of the oldest holy days in Christian history, is celebrated in the first week of the new year, customarily on January 6. Epiphany is Greek for manifestation and refers to God's presence being made manifest, or shown, in the world. The symbolic candlelight of Epiphany is a welcome and hopeful sign in this sometimes frozen and dark time of year. Historically, the waters of baptism have also played a significant role in Epiphany celebrations. Following are some suggestions for simple rituals and activities that extend the themes and symbols of Epiphany from New Year's Eve into the days and weeks to follow. This section offers ways to help you ground your family in God as the New Year begins and to bring a spiritual focus to your celebrations of the Martin Luther King, Jr., holiday and Valentine's Day.

BLESSING THE HOME

Ancient New Year's House Blessing

You will need:
   About five minutes
   Sidewalk or blackboard chalk

• SUGGESTED SCRIPTURE: Ezekiel 11:19; Isaiah 43:18-19;
                   Jeremiah 31:31-33; Luke 5:36-38;
                   Matthew 3:13-17

In the Middle Ages it was customary for families to gather at midnight, open the front door to let in the New Year, and open the back door to let out the old. Another tradition at the time was to write a blessing above the door with chalk on the evening before Epiphany. Here, these two practices are combined in a simple and brief ritual for families with young children.

Choose a time when the family is together, perhaps before or after a meal on New Year's Eve, New Year's Day or Epiphany, which is January 6 or sometimes celebrated on the nearest Sunday. Explain that the family is going to say good-bye to the old year and hello to the New Year, and ask God to bless the home.

After opening the back and front doors, stand for a moment between the two. Perhaps you'll feel a breath of air moving through as one year passes into the next. Close the back door; go to the front and with chalk write 20+C+M+B+(year, for example 05 or 06) above the door, or on the doorstep. The numbers signify the date of the coming year and the letters traditionally stand for the names of the Three Kings who followed the star to bring gifts to the newborn Jesus in Bethlehem. Their names are said to have been Casper, Melchior and Balthasar. Others say the letters stand for *Christus Mansionem Benedictat,* or "Christ bless this home."

End with one of the above-mentioned suggested Scripture readings or a short prayer such as the following:

> Loving God, we thank you for all the blessings of the past year, especially (name). Please continue to bless us, our loved ones and our home throughout the coming year. Amen.

Blessing the Home with Water

You will need:

About fifteen minutes

Water (Your parish may have holy water available in the church. You may want to ask your priest to bless some water for you, or you may use water from the faucet.)

Small evergreen branch (Perhaps snipped from the Christmas tree, or something similar to use for sprinkling water, like a feather.)

• SUGGESTED SCRIPTURE: Isaiah 41:18; John 4:4-29; 9:10-14

Gather the family at the front door of your apartment or home and begin with a Scripture reading or an opening prayer such as the following:

God bless all who enter this door in the coming year. Bless us as we come and go. Keep us safely in your care, and may our hearts and our door always be open to offer hospitality to all.

Then dip the branch in the water and sprinkle the door. Walk through your home stopping in each room to bless and sprinkle. Take turns, both sprinkling and speaking the blessing, giving everyone a chance to participate. You may include the bathroom, hallway and even closets. The children won't want to see any holy water left over!

Blessing the Home with Light

You will need:

About fifteen minutes

Candle with holder to catch dripping wax

Matches or lighter

Song, hymn or music such as:

"This Little Light of Mine" (African American Spiritual)

"Joy to the World," lyrics by Isaac Watts (1719) and music by Llowell Mason (1836)

"Amazing Grace," lyrics John Newton (1779) and music by James P. Carrell and David S. Clayton (1831)

"Praise God From Whom All Blessings Flow," lyrics by Thomas Ken (1674) and lyrics by Louis Bourgeois (1551)

"Lord of all Hopefulness," lyrics by Jan Struther ©1931
(Jan Struther is a pseudonym for Joyce Maxtone Graham)
"We are Many Parts," lyrics and music by Marty Haugen ©1980

• Suggested Scripture: Genesis 1:3-5; Psalm 27:1; Matthew 5:14:16

Begin by gathering the family at the front door or in the main room of your home. Choose a reader and someone to light and blow out the candle.

Reader: This is the day the Lord has made, let us rejoice and be glad.

All: This is the day the Lord has made, let us rejoice and be glad.

Light candle

Reader: Light of Christ, shine in our hearts and home. Bless us and this home throughout the coming year. May your love enkindle in us compassion and justice. May it illuminate all we think, say and do. May your Spirit guide us in wisdom and truth and bring us to everlasting life.

All: Amen.

Process through the home carrying the candle and singing a hymn or song of praise. If your family doesn't know a song, you may choose to play an appropriate tape or CD. End in the kitchen or dining room and share hot chocolate and cookies. Finish with this traditional prayer or make up your own.

> We give Thee thanks for all Thy benefits, Almighty God, who liveth and reigneth forever. May the souls of the faithful departed, through the mercy of God, rest in peace. Amen.

Blow out the candle.

Single Mother's Home Blessing

• Suggested Scripture: Wisdom 7:7-12; 22:30

In some families it is traditional for the New Year's Blessing to be performed by the family matriarch. Each of the previous rituals can be adapted in this way. Invite grandmothers, aunts or other women who are important in your life to share this day with you. Perhaps a single woman in your parish would welcome this opportunity to celebrate with a family.

BLESS THIS MESS

A swirl of conflicting feelings threatened to overwhelm me one January just after we moved into our new home. The eighty-year-old house was my dream home with its craftsman character and a huge shade tree in the front yard, but it needed a lot of work ranging from new mortar on the foundation to wallpaper removal in every room. We had just moved away from a wonderful support system of friends to a town where we hardly knew anyone. And on top of all that, I was expecting our third child.

It was in the midst of these circumstances that we gathered our family and began the annual ritual of blessing our home. The ceremony gave me space to voice my gratitude for our new house and to replace my fears and anxiety with an attitude of faith in God's providence. Simply taking a few moments to focus on the blessings of the moment gave me renewed energy to face the work that lay ahead.

Since that first blessing in our home, this tradition has become a favorite for the whole family. It's fun for the children, marching around and throwing water with no threat of reprisal. And it's the strong medicine of faith, too. I saw it in the eyes of my youngest son the year he was five and heard it in his earnest words as he led us in prayer in his bedroom.

"God, bless this room and everyone who comes in and my stuffed animals Stevie Bunny, Nick, Swoop and Gecko."

He was followed by the muttered words of our teenager.

"God, bless this room and help me get a good night's sleep. I'll do my homework sometime tomorrow."

Sometimes I'm tempted to censor my children's prayers, like when they are blessing the bathroom. When I am blessing rooms, my tendency is to be long-winded and holy-sounding. Luckily our family is balanced by my husband's sense of humor. The children seem to take after him with relish, and I'm left hoping God has a similar funny bone. I must admit my most enthusiastic "Amen" came the time my daughter prayed, "God, bless this room and help me clean it when it gets messy."

Blessing is not magic. We do not make something blessed; rather we recognize and draw attention to the holiness that has already been infused by God. We notice the sacred present in the sometimes mundane and mostly ordinary daily life. We open our eyes to our part in God's creative work.

Despite a New Year's blessing, life in our home will most likely continue to be messy. Interactions will sometimes be less than loving and motivations less than pure. But this simple annual custom serves to remind us that in the midst of daily family life, there exists a spark of the holy.

CLEARING AWAY CLUTTER

• SUGGESTED SCRIPTURE: Matthew 6:19-21; 19:16-26;
Acts 2:42-47; 17:25b-28a

"Do not store up for yourselves treasures on earth...."—MATTHEW 6:19

One way to extend the idea of house blessing into the following weeks of the year is to clear away clutter in your home. Getting rid of stuff you don't really need can bring a sense of freedom and peace of mind. You'll spend less time cleaning and caring for items. Rooms will have a more spacious and tidy feel and you'll have fewer distractions. Reducing clutter in your home can help clear your mind, and you'll be able to focus on what matters most: relationships, spirituality and creativity. Here are some suggestions:

• Cancel subscriptions for magazines you don't read.

• Give away clothes that no longer fit or that you haven't worn in the last year.

• Go through kitchen cupboards and take out items you rarely or never use.

• Give away small appliances that initially seemed efficient but turned out to be more trouble than help.

• Clear out the cabinets of coffee mugs sporting cute sayings, but are just taking space on a shelf.

The process of sorting through your possessions and eliminating what you no longer need may be easier if everyone helps. Sometimes it can even be fun. Here are a few strategies to help you get started.

1. The Stuffed Animal Draft

Ever feel you're being overrun by Teletubbies, Pooh Bears and Beanie Babies? Sometimes I swear they're multiplying in the night. My husband is a big sports fan, often watching the NFL and NBA drafts live on television, so the "stuffed animal draft" seemed a natural solution for us. We put all the plush toys in a big pile in the middle of the room. Five animals per child seemed more than reasonable, so they went five rounds choosing cuddly-creatures they couldn't live without. Then, tearfully, they said good-bye to those left over.

The "draft" can be used with toys in general, books or anything you have in abundance. We also used it when our coffee mug shelf recently began to runneth over.

2. The Two-for-One Art and School Paper Challenge

I developed this strategy while helping my daughter clean her room. We discovered a pile of papers under her bed that would put a government bureaucracy to shame. I insisted every one could not be a treasure and asked her to throw away two for every one she saved. In the end, we managed to press all her masterpieces into one shirt box.

By limiting the children to one shirt box per school year, the papers seem manageable. By third or fourth grade, they no longer seem so attached to most of their work. I've purchased one large cardboard file box for each of my children as a special "save" box. These contain everything from artwork to birthday cards from Grandma, award certificates and even small toys, once treasured and now outgrown. This seems a good way to both save things, and limit the amount. My oldest is now a senior in high school, and his box is not quite full.

Cheryl, a mother of five, says sorting through school papers can also be a great time to talk with your child about how much they have grown and changed in the past year. "It's a special time alone with each child," says Cheryl. "My kids love it."

3. Sharing With Others

In the book of Acts we read about the early Christian communities sharing everything in common and giving to each according to his need. This might seem unworkable in our modern lives, but it is worth reflecting upon. Thinking "out of the box," you may come up with ways of sharing with friends and neighbors that allow you to own fewer things and at the same time strengthen relationships.

For instance, in a suburban cul-de-sac, does each family need to own a lawn mower? With some planning, perhaps give-and-take, and a willingness to resolve disagreements in good faith, several families could share a lawn mower. We bought our house from a man and wife in their mid-eighties and discovered that they had been sharing a snow blower with an older couple across the street for years. Tens of thousands of Europeans participate in car-sharing arrangements, and now the idea has taken root in several major American cities.

Families can also share housework or lawn care. When I was at home full-time with young children, two other mothers and I decided to share cooking responsibilities. We formed a dinner co-op, taking turns once a week cooking the evening meal for all three families. Though we had one busy afternoon in the kitchen, we had two other afternoons when we didn't even need to think about what to cook for dinner. The arrangement felt risky at first. What if we didn't like what they cooked?

One of the first meals we received was almost too spicy for me to eat. We had to communicate clearly and honestly, be flexible about dinnertime and become somewhat humble about our cooking. But the dinner co-op proved a great success. The greatest reward was that strong friendships developed between our families. We felt a sense of connection and caring that we believe expressed God's presence in daily life. For us it was a way of carrying Sunday Eucharist over into the remainder of the week.

EPIPHANY

• SUGGESTED SCRIPTURE: Matthew 2:1-12; Mark 1:9-11; John 2:1-11

One of the oldest Christian celebrations comes in the first week of the New Year—Epiphany, January 6. The day celebrates three events in the life of Christ: three kings led by a star to visit the baby Jesus in Bethlehem, Jesus turning water into wine at a wedding in Cana and Jesus' Baptism in the Jordan River.

In its early centuries the church baptized new members on the eve of Epiphany. The Byzantine Rite of the church celebrates the Solemn Blessing of the Water that night. In ancient times people processed to the nearest river or stream where the priest performed the ritual blessing of the water, and people filled dippers and carried the water to their homes as a reminder of divine protection throughout the year. A candelabrum holding three candles was lit during the celebration to signify the Blessed Trinity made known in Jesus' Baptism in the waters of the Jordan. You can use these same symbols in simple ways in your home to invoke the deeper meaning of God's presence in your family life.

Through the centuries, both light and water have been important elements in the rituals of Epiphany. Light is an apt metaphor for God's presence radiating out into the world. That presence also shines inward and is revealed to each member of the family in the quiet of his or her own heart. Recognizing the light of God in ourselves, each other and in the daily routine at home sometimes takes extra effort, time and planning. But the rewards are beyond measure as we grow in faith and love, and God empowers us to go out from the home in service to the wider world.

ACTIVITIES FOR EPIPHANY

Kings' Crowns

You will need:
>   Thirty minutes to one hour
>   One large sheet of construction paper for each person
>   Scissors
>   Crayons or markers
>   Stapler or tape
>   Children's Bible or storybook about the Three Kings bringing gifts to Jesus
>   Optional: small wrapped gift for each child

1. Begin by explaining to the children that you are celebrating the three kings bringing gifts to Jesus. You will be making crowns and thinking about what gift you can give Jesus.

2. Help each child cut the construction paper into a wide strip long enough to go around their head. They can cut a zigzag or any shape they like. You may have to tape or staple two strips together to make the crown.

3. Let the children use markers or crayons to decorate the paper. For older children, you may want to have glue and sequins, glitter, beads, etc. with which to decorate the crowns. (Adults present should also make crowns.)

4. Fasten the crown into a circle with tape or staples.

5. When the crowns are finished, place them on your heads and read the story of the three kings from the Bible or storybook. Some children may want to act out the story.

Children understand that gold is precious. You may want to explain that the other gifts, frankincense and myrrh, were also expensive and rare. They were strong-smelling gum resins from African and Asian trees used in perfume and burned as incense—ancient-day air fresheners of a sort.

Ask your children what gift they might offer Jesus. Prompt them by sharing something you could give, perhaps the gift of good listening, help with chores or remembering to use kind words. If you like, end the celebration by offering the children small wrapped gifts.

Buñuelos—For a Latin American Epiphany

In Spanish-speaking countries many children have not grown up with the custom of Santa Claus bringing presents on Christmas. Rather, they received gifts on Epiphany to commemorate the three wise men who followed the star in the East to bring offerings and pay homage to the Christ Child. Sometimes children left their shoes outside the door the eve of January 6, where they would find them the next morning filled with gifts or coins. Epiphany festivities often included a piñata which the children took turns whacking with a stick until it broke open, spilling out treats. Some communities marked the day with a parade, and most everyone celebrated with a feast of special holiday foods. The following recipe is for sweet fried bread some Mexican families enjoy on Epiphany.

This recipe makes about two dozen buñuelos, a lightly fried Mexican treat that predates the Spaniards. Topped with frosting or cinnamon sugar it makes a special sweet treat that will please adults and kids alike. Children may enjoy mixing and rolling the dough, but an adult is needed for the job of deep-frying the buñuelos.

You will need:

> About one hour
> 3½ cups flour
> 1 cup butter (two sticks)
> 1 teaspoon salt
> ½ cup milk
> 1 teaspoon baking powder
> 2 eggs, beaten
> 1½ cups (see directions below) vegetable shortening or
>   vegetable oil
> *Capa de Azucar y Canela* (cinnamon-sugar topping for buñuelos)

Combine in bowl and set aside:

> 1½ cups sugar
> 2 teaspoons cinnamon

1. Combine flour, salt, baking powder and sugar in a large mixing bowl and cut in butter.

2. Add eggs and milk to flour mixture and work mixture into dough. Knead dough until it is smooth and elastic. Form dough into balls the size of an egg. Cover dough and set aside for 15 minutes.

3. Roll each ball of dough into a circle 4 inches in diameter. Cut a small hole in center of each circle. Place circles of dough between single layers of waxed paper until all are rolled flat and ready to be deep-fried.

4. Heat approximately 2 inches of shortening in a heavy saucepan (preferably cast-iron skillet) at medium-high heat.

5. Fry buñuelos until they are puffed, turning once to brown on both sides.

6. Remove buñuelos from pan and drain on paper towels.

7. Sprinkle the buñuelos with a cinnamon-sugar topping (see recipe above) and serve warm.

MARTIN LUTHER KING, JR., DAY: WORKING FOR JUSTICE

- SUGGESTED SCRIPTURE: Isaiah 26:4-7; Micah 6:8; Luke 6:43-44

"If you close your ear to the cry of the poor, you will cry out and not be heard."—PROVERBS 21:13

The third Monday in January is a national holiday honoring America's most prominent civil rights activist, Doctor Martin Luther King, Jr. In addition, King's birthday, January 15, is observed in more than one hundred nations around the world because of his work for justice and equality and his example of nonviolent resistance to oppression.

King inspired people of all races as he preached against racism and for unconditional love and forgiveness. Despite beatings, imprisonment, the bombing of his home and continuing threats against his life, King remained committed to peaceful resistance, saying "I believe that unarmed truth and unconditional love will have the final word." King was assassinated while supporting a sanitation workers' strike in Memphis, Tennessee, on April 4, 1968.

The Martin Luther King holiday is a good time to talk to your children about the need for Christian people to work for justice. Pope John Paul II wrote in his "The Hundredth Year" documents that "love for others, and especially for the poor, is made concrete by promoting justice. The life and words of Jesus and the teaching of his Church call us to serve those in need and to work actively for social and economic justice." He noted specifically that this commitment begins in the family.

When parents are busy changing diapers, cooking meals, attending school events and working for a living, it's a challenge to find time and energy to even think about issues like social and economic justice. Few of us are called to go out and lead a March on Washington like Doctor King, but through our baptism we are called to act for justice in the circumstances of our own daily lives. Here are some suggestions to help you do that.

1. Be just in disciplining your children. If you realize you have made a mistake by acting harshly out of anger or having expectations that were too high, admit it and apologize. If you realize you have been preoccupied, distracted or tired and become too lenient, apologize and explain that you will be making a better effort to enforce the family rules consistently.

2. Take advantage of your child's experiences to teach about justice. Incidents on the playground or in the schoolroom make great opportunities. Is a child being left out because he speaks with an accent? Or is another teased because she gets poor grades? Another ignored because she uses a wheelchair? Young children can understand the unfairness of situations like these. Show them they have a choice in how they react.

3. Stand up in the face of injustice. We teach our children to do it when we have the courage to do it ourselves. Admit that this can be hard to do and may take practice. Role-play situations so your children can try saying the words out loud. For instance, "I don't like it when you call José names. It's not fair."

4. Give your children tools to handle strong emotions in nonviolent ways. If you are angry, or you see that your child is angry, call a time-out and wait until everyone has cooled off before you try solving the problem. Demonstrate how to use words to work out disputes.

5. Look for children's books about people like Doctor Martin Luther King, Jr., who have acted for justice. Suggestions: Dorothy Day, Archbishop Oscar Romero, Saint Elizabeth Ann Seton, Saint Catherine Drexel, Blessed Damien, Saint Martin de Porres.

6. As a family, take part in a peaceful demonstration such as a Martin Luther King Day rally, a pro-life march or a candlelight vigil for victims of war or terrorism. Marches like Church World Service's annual CROP WALK are family-friendly demonstrations that make a statement for justice as well as raise money to fight hunger around the world.

VALENTINE'S DAY: NOT JUST FOR LOVERS

"No one has greater love than this, to lay down one's life for one's friend."—JOHN 15:13

There are varying stories about the origin of Valentine's Day. One of the most well-known tells us the day was named for a priest imprisoned and killed by the Roman government because he was Christian.

As the story goes, Valentine became a friend of his jailer's daughter. When the time came for his execution, he sent her a farewell message signed, "From your Valentine." He died in A.D. 269 on February 14, the day ancient Romans honored Juno, the goddess of women and marriage.

This friendship between a young unnamed girl and a priest known for his kindness, faith and courage can be a model for celebrating Valentine's Day in the spirit of Jesus.

This is an ideal date for married couples to take time to nurture their relationship. It's an important reminder that love needs feeding and care to thrive. The holiday can be painful and lonely for single people. It is a wonderful opportunity for us to reach out to those who lack love or even companionship in their lives.

Valentine Activities for Families with Young Children

Choose a small act of kindness you can do for someone who may be lonely on this holiday. For example, a widowed neighbor, a single relative or friend, a divorced member of your parish or a stranger in a nursing home. Sending a store-bought valentine may be all you have time for, but it could mean a lot to someone who rarely gets anything but junk mail. If you have more time, considering making a few homemade valentines with your children or baking and delivering cookies.

Valentine Activities for Families with Older Children

Consider sending Valentine's Day greetings to teenagers staying at a homeless shelter. You could add real warmth to your holiday wishes by attaching a gift of a pair of socks or gloves. Ask friends or your church youth group to join your efforts.

A visit to prisoners at your local jail or prison befits the spirit of the original Saint Valentine and has the potential to have a huge impact on your teenager. Visiting prisoners is one of the corporal works of mercy listed in the Gospel of Matthew in which Jesus said, "Truly, I tell you, just as you did it to one of the least of these who are members of my family, you did it to me" (Matthew 25:40).

However, this is likely to take a bit more paperwork in modern times than it did in Jesus' time. You will mostly likely have to undergo a background check that could take more than two weeks. If your parish does not have a jail ministry team, consider linking up with a prison chaplain who will be able to advise you about how best to interact with those incarcerated. Going along on regular rounds or attending a prescheduled Mass with the chaplain might be easiest for first-time visitors.

Perhaps these ideas seem too difficult or time consuming for your busy family. If so, pick one small thing you can do to celebrate Valentine's Day in the spirit of Christian love. A small step is better than no step at all. The germ of an idea may take root and grow.

Valentine Activities for Parents

Couples who regularly spend time alone together enjoy more satisfying relationships. Scheduling a regular date night helps married couples maintain a deeper level of intimacy. If you and your spouse don't have the date night habit, Valentine's Day is a great time to start.

A romantic evening does not have to include an expensive dinner out or a huge block of time. My most memorable Valentine's celebration with my husband cost almost nothing and lasted exactly two hours. That's because the main provision for the night was a babysitting exchange I made with another mom I met through my daughter's preschool. I baked my husband's favorite meal, lasagna. While it was in the oven, I dropped the children off at my friend's house. Arriving back home, I set the dining room table for two, lit candles, opened a bottle of wine, turned on music and waited for my husband to come home. Two hours later the children came home to very happy parents!

2

LENT
Growing in Christ

• SUGGESTED SCRIPTURE: Matthew 26–27; Mark 14–15; Luke 22–23;
John 18–19

Lent is a time set aside for spiritual growth and renewal in order to prepare for Easter. In this season we recommit ourselves to the disci-
plines of prayer, fasting and almsgiving, an old word meaning sharing
with the needy. We make a special effort to refocus our lives on the
gospel. Through the rituals of Holy Week we accompany Jesus on his
journey to Calvary, and we strive to die to our sins in the hope of rising to new life on Easter.

The season of Lent includes the forty days before Easter beginning Ash Wednesday and excluding Sundays. In biblical language the
number forty shows up often, not as a literal number, but implying an
amount of time that is significant in some way. It is like a road sign saying "pay attention, something important is about to happen." For
example, the Israelites wandered forty years before arriving in the
Promised Land, and Gospel writers say Jesus fasted forty days in the
desert before beginning his public ministry.

The word Lent comes from a variety of Anglo-Saxon and Germanic words meaning spring, a time budding with new life and hope.
Our spiritual exercises of prayer and fasting can be characterized with
a lightheartedness that acknowledges that though we sometimes fail
to live up to our expectations, we know that Christ lives and that his
rising from death has conquered sin for all time. The following are
some ideas to help you and your family mark the passage of Lent from
Ash Wednesday to Holy Saturday.

MARDI GRAS

Mardi Gras, French for "Fat Tuesday," is celebrated the day before Ash Wednesday. In many regions of the world, Mardi Gras festivities last several days to a week with parties, parades and feasts which have been the custom since the Middle Ages. At that time Fat Tuesday was the last chance to eat meats, eggs and dairy foods to make ready for the strict lenten fast.

In England it was traditional to mark the day with a pancake supper, as pancakes were a good way to use up milk, eggs and butter. Families can borrow this tradition as a simple way to celebrate the day. Take time during the meal to explain the history of Mardi Gras and the Christian practice of fasting. (For more on fasting see, "Families that Fast Together...") If you have more time and energy, gather bells, whistles, balloons and party hats for a festive atmosphere and one last party before Lent.

ASH WEDNESDAY

Most churches hold services on Ash Wednesday to mark the beginning of Lent. It is tradition to burn the palms from last year's Palm Sunday and use the ashes to mark people's foreheads with a cross. In biblical times people smeared their faces with ashes when a loved one died. They also dumped ashes on their heads as a sign of repentance before God. The cross of ashes is a sign of Jesus' victory over sin and death. If you cannot make it to your parish Ash Wednesday service, you can plan your own ritual at home. Following is an Ash Wednesday family prayer and several other ideas you might use to mark the day.

Ash Wednesday Family Prayer Service

- SUGGESTED SCRIPTURE: Isaiah 58:6-8; Tobit 4:7; Matthew 6:1-4, 5-8, 16-18

You will need:
> About half an hour
> Last year's palm fronds (optional)
> Several pieces of paper
> Metal bowl or large ash tray
> Matches or lighter

1. If you have last year's palm fronds, prepare ahead of time by snipping them into small pieces and placing them in the fire safe bowl.

2. Gather the family (preferably outdoors) and choose someone to open with prayer, someone to be leader and someone to light the fire.

3. Begin with a prayer such as:

> God, we gather tonight as Lent begins to ask your blessing on our family and on all people of the world. Open our hearts to your love, and help us to grow in holiness this season.

Leader: Let's take a moment to think about something that will help us to grow more like Jesus this Lent. Could we be more willing to share our toys? Be more patient? Be more helpful by doing extra chores? Commit to more prayer time or to Bible study? Or give up something like TV or dessert? Let's promise to do one special thing for Lent.

(If you have palms to burn, write down everyone's promise on a sheet of paper to post on the refrigerator or another prominent place. During Lent family members can check in with each other once a week and encourage one another. If you don't have palms to burn, write each person's promise on a separate sheet of paper. Crunch up the papers and place them in the fire safe bowl.)

4. Let an adult carefully light the palms or papers on fire and pray:

Leader: Our prayers and promises rise to heaven as smoke rises from this fire. We offer ourselves to God as we are, with both our failings and our triumphs. Bless these ashes, God. May they be a reminder of our need to turn from sin and seek new life in you.

5. When the ashes are cool, each family member takes some on a finger and makes the sign of the cross with the ashes on another person's forehead saying, "Turn away from sin and seek new life in Christ." Continue until everyone has given and received ashes.

6. Close with a prayer or song.

> Glory be to the Father, and to the Son and to the Holy Spirit. As it was in the beginning, is now, and ever shall be, world without end. Amen.

Suggested Songs:
"Ashes," lyrics and music by Tom Conroy (New Dawn Music)
"Turn to Me," lyrics and music John Foley, S.J. (New Dawn Music)

Other Ash Wednesday and Lenten Activities

1. Use a purple tablecloth on Ash Wednesday and throughout Lent. Purple is the liturgical color that reminds us that it is a season of prayer and penance. Inexpensive plastic tablecloths are available at party supply stores, or check the fabric store for purple cloth. Twice I've found cheap remnants of royal purple fabric that didn't even need hemming.

2. For breakfast serve hot cross buns, which are traditional food for Ash Wednesday and Good Friday. The buns are made from a sweet dough with dried currants, and decorated with a crosscut filled with frosting. They represent Jesus' death on the cross and the "sweetness" of growing nearer to him through fasting and prayer.

3. Gather the whole family for a simple meal of bread and broth in the spirit of Ash Wednesday fasting. Light a candle to emphasize it is a special occasion.

4. Take time to talk about what each family member might do for Lent. Write down on a piece of paper what each person commits to do and post it in a prominent spot, perhaps on the refrigerator.

FAMILIES THAT FAST TOGETHER...

There's a story about Catholic school children reciting the Ten Commandments. When they were finished, a little boy said, "Wait, we forgot one."

"Which?" asked the teacher.

"Thou shalt give up candy for Lent."

I remember reaching an age, probably about eight, when I rebelled against this lenten practice. I'm still not sweet on the idea. But I have come to appreciate the value of some type of lenten fast.

Fasting is not meant to be a way of punishing ourselves; rather, it's making a small sacrifice to join with the sacrifice Christ made on the cross.

Fasting is also like an exercise class for our self-discipline muscle. I tell my children it's a way of practicing "not getting everything you want" or "not having things your way." This practice in small things can give us the strength and endurance to be Christ-like when harder times come.

Fasting together as a family can be rewarding. You can encourage one another, and even if you are not completely successful the whole family will benefit from trying.

Start by sharing with your children any experiences you might have had as a child giving up something for Lent. Talk about whether the practice was meaningful for you. In simple terms try to explain why you are fasting this Lent, and why you want other family members to join you.

You could talk about Jesus fasting forty days in the desert and your desire to grow to be more like him. Or you could explain how fasting whets the appetite for a feast.

I think it's best to let children decide for themselves what they want to give up. That way it's more likely to be meaningful for them. But I'm not above using gentle parental persuasion. One method is to help them narrow the field to two choices then urge them to pick one.

Ways to Fast

1. Fast from drinks except water (and milk if needed for nutrition). This is a way to be in solidarity with others who have less. Billions of people in the world have nothing to drink but water. And their water is often contaminated by human, animal and chemical waste. Even though Americans have the purest and most accessible tap water in the world, statistics from the beverage industry show that since 1989 Americans have been consuming more soda pop than water. At a growing rate, Americans drink commercial beverages packaged in single-use containers, and transported over long distances. This habit requires a huge outlay of the world's resources.

2. Fast from TV, computer and video games. If unplugging electronics completely sounds too difficult for your family, try cutting your time to half. Double your benefit by increasing the time you spend together as a family. Play board games or charades. Take a walk together, tell jokes or share stories while looking at family photo albums.

3. Fast from criticism. This is hard because sometimes we don't even realize we've been critical until the words are out of our mouth. Try this. Agree on a secret sign, such as tugging an earlobe, to quietly signal someone they are being critical. Family members commit to only make the sign in good faith, and to zip their lips without question if they are given the signal. This can help both kids and adults to be more conscious of their words.

4. Fast from overwork and over-commitment. If you or your spouse tend to work overtime or have demanding volunteer activities, Lent can be a good time to take a break. Cut back to give yourself and your family several free hours a week. Use the time to relax together as a family with no set agenda.

PRETZEL PARTY: A LENTEN TWIST

Teaching children to practice self-denial can require the strength of Samson, the endurance of Job and the wisdom of Solomon. If the job feels overwhelming, try this project. It's a simple, fun way to introduce children to the ideas of lenten prayer and fasting, and will help make your kitchen a holy place where faith rises and grows like yeasty dough.

Start with this easy recipe for soft pretzels made in a bag to minimize mess. Little hands can easily knead the dough. Older children may be interested to learn the unusual history of pretzels. The salty snack we know may have begun as a lenten food in ancient times. References to pretzels appear in manuscripts dating back to the fifth century.

At that time and up through the Middle Ages, Christians observed strict fasts during Lent. They gave up meat, cheese, milk, butter and eggs in the forty days before Easter. A staple of that limited diet was bread made of nothing but flour, water and salt, the forerunner of today's pretzels.

Early Christians often stood or kneeled with arms crossed over their chests while praying. Eventually, as a reminder to pray during Lent, they twisted their simple bread dough to resemble praying arms. The bread was called "little arms"—brachellae, later brezel and finally pretzel.

Bake your pretzels and join the long tradition of fasting to prepare for Easter. Heat vegetable broth to accompany the pretzels for a simple meal. At the table engage your children in conversation about hunger in your community and the world. Explain that many people eat a meager diet every day because of poverty, war or natural disaster. Invite the children to pray in thanksgiving for the wide selection of food we enjoy.

Recipe for Soft Pretzels Made in a Bag

You will need:
>About two hours, plus mealtime
>1 large plastic bag with locking seal
>1 cup warm water
>1 package fast-rising yeast
>2 tablespoons sugar
>1 teaspoon salt
>1 tablespoon vegetable oil
>3+ cups flour, divided
>1 egg
>Pastry brush or several sheets of paper towel
>Coarse salt, poppy seeds or sesame seeds
>Canned vegetable broth or bouillon, ¾ cup per person

1. Put in bag: 1 cup flour, yeast, sugar and water. Close and seal.

2. Knead bag with your fingers to blend the ingredients. Let rest for 10 minutes.

3. Add to the bag 1 cup flour, salt and oil.

4. Knead dough in bag until flour is well blended. Gradually add small amounts of flour and knead until the dough pulls away from sides of the bag. Dough should form a ball. Continue kneading 5 to 10 more minutes.

5. Remove dough and place in large bowl.

6. Cover with plastic wrap and let rise in a warm place 30-40 minutes.

7. Preheat oven to 375° at least 15-16 minutes before bake time.

8. Turn dough onto lightly floured board. Divide dough in half; divide each half into 6 equal pieces. Roll each piece into a 20-inch long rope. Shape each rope into a pretzel by grabbing both ends of the long roll, twisting them, and laying the ends flat across the base of the rope.

9. Set 2 inches apart on lightly greased baking sheet.

10. Beat egg with fork. Use pastry brush or paper towel to coat top of pretzels with beaten egg.

11. Sprinkle with salt or seeds.

12. Bake 15-20 minutes. Remove from baking sheets and cool on wire racks.

Makes 12 large soft pretzels. Serve with vegetable broth prepared according to package directions.

MAKING FORGIVENESS A FAMILY HABIT

Sometimes we have the idea that a loving Christian family is one in which everyone gets along perfectly. In reality, even the most loving homes are places where we live in such close quarters that over time our rough edges are exposed. This gives us the opportunity to learn that we all need forgiveness.

As we are not born knowing how to love, neither do we naturally know how to forgive. The family is our first and most important school in these virtues. We parents will probably have to ask forgiveness of our children a thousand times before they begin to take responsibility for their failures and learn to ask forgiveness.

When forgiveness happens routinely in a family, children readily understand and are able to accept forgiveness of sin from God and the community. They will not see the sacrament of reconciliation as something negative or scary. They will already have experienced many times the joy and healing that comes with admitting fault and being forgiven.

On a daily basis the words "I'm sorry" and "I forgive you" said sincerely are enough to heal wounds in family relationships. Accompanied by a hug, a smile or some other gesture of caring or restitution, these simple words work wonders. Serious hurts and larger breaches of trust take a proportionate time to heal. Do not force children to say they are sorry. If children see reconciliation modeled, they will begin to apologize when they are developmentally able to do so. Ritualizing contrition and forgiveness can be helpful in that it gives words and feelings a concrete expression.

A family reconciliation ritual does not have to be a big production to be worthwhile. Families have different styles and needs. People express feelings in different ways. Experiment to find out what is meaningful for you and your loved ones. Every couple of weeks, once a month or a few times a year take a few moments at mealtime or bedtime to ritualize forgiveness. Lent and Advent are times of penitence in the church, so make appropriate times to focus on repentance and forgiveness in the family.

Practicing Forgiveness with Young Children

Gather, perhaps holding your child on your lap, and begin with a simple prayer or Scripture reading.

"Love one another as I have loved you."—JOHN 15:12

> Dear Jesus, we want to love each other. We're sorry that sometimes we fail to follow your example. Please help us be more like you. Amen.

Parents, speak your apologies aloud. For instance, "I am sorry that I spoke sharply to you today when I asked you to pick up your toys. I ask God, and I ask you, to forgive me."

Then ask your child, "Is there anything you are sorry for?" You may coach by asking questions. "What about when you hit the baby today? Was that a loving thing to do?" Do not force your child to apologize. If he is not ready, simply continue to model this skill.

Show your forgiveness of each other with a hug. End with a prayer thanking God for loving you and forgiving you.

Forgiveness Stones*

* This family reconciliation ritual is not appropriate for children younger than about eight years old.

You will need:
Twenty minutes or longer
Bible
Some reminder of Jesus such as a small crucifix,
    statue or picture
Candle and matches
Stones

1. Place your crucifix, statue or picture of Jesus on a table next to the unlit candle.

2. Gather the family and begin with prayer such as:

> God, you sent your only Son, Jesus, to live a human life like us, to live on earth and show us how to love and forgive. Through his death and Resurrection we are saved from our sins. We try to follow his example of love and forgiveness, but we sometimes fail. We are here together as a family to admit our mistakes, to ask forgiveness and to become more united in love. We ask your blessing. Amen.

3. Read John 8:3-11

4. Talk briefly about this Gospel reading. Though children will not understand the sin of adultery in this story, make sure they take in the point that no one is perfect. All of us fail from time to time. Explain that now you will go for a short walk outside so each person can find a small stone which will be his or her "forgiveness stone," a symbol of our need for forgiveness.

5. When you come back, explain that like the characters in the Gospel stories, you will each think about the fact that you are not without sin and in turn drop your stone at the feet of Jesus.

6. Parents, let's take a moment to remember the times we have failed. Maybe we have hurt one another, been impatient, unkind, unwilling to share or have let our anger take hold.

7. A parent might now take the lead in voicing acknowledgment of failure, apologizing and asking forgiveness. While speaking, the parent drops a forgiveness stone at the foot of the cross or other symbol of Jesus.

8. When all family members have placed their stones and voiced their need for forgiveness, light the candle as a sign of God's forgiveness and healing shining on the family. Join hands and pray the Our Father together.

- ADDITIONAL SCRIPTURE ON FORGIVENESS: Psalm 51:1-2; 103:8-10; 145:8; Isaiah 49:15-16; Luke 11:4; Colossians 3:12-17; Ephesians 4:32

JUGGLING HOLY WEEK AND HOMEWORK

- SUGGESTED SCRIPTURE: Exodus 12:21-30

Holy Week is the most sacred time of year for Christians, but it is sometimes challenging for families to focus on the meaning of these important days. The prevailing culture does not pause to mark Jesus' last days on earth. Unlike Christmas, there's no school vacation. If you are juggling the kids' homework, piano lessons, sports and church services, it helps to look ahead at the calendar and make plans in advance.

The church offers a powerful way of moving through this climax of the liturgical year in the Easter Triduum. It begins with Holy Thursday Mass and continues through Good Friday service and Easter Vigil on Holy Saturday Eve. Experiencing these celebrations with your family and parish community can be the height of the liturgical year.

For single-parent families, those with several young children or others with busy teenagers it can difficult, even impossible, to get the family together for Holy Week services. If your family cannot attend the Triduum, you may want to consider a simple celebration at home. The examples on the following page, one for each of the three holy days, can serve as starting points. Adapt them to fit the needs of your family.

Holy Thursday: Washing of the Feet

• SUGGESTED SCRIPTURE: John 13:1-15

You will need:
    Twenty minutes to one hour
    Bible
    Large bowl or basin of warm water
    Two towels

1. Gather in the main living space of your home. Spread one towel on the floor and place the bowl of water on it. Keep the second towel handy for drying feet later. Begin with the Sign of the Cross and a simple prayer asking that your hearts be open to God's Word.

2. Read aloud John 13:1-15. For young families it's helpful to use a Bible written especially for children. Explain that in Jesus' time there were no sidewalks or paved streets. People wore sandals and their feet got very dirty and smelly from the dust and mud. At the time, only a servant or slave would stoop to wash someone else's feet. Ask the children how they might have reacted if they were the disciples whose feet Jesus washed. Explain that you will wash each other's feet as a sign that family members will try to serve one another in love as Jesus did.

3. Move a chair near the bowl of water. Start with the youngest person sitting with his or her feet in the water, while another family member kneels, washes and dries that one's feet. Each person should take a turn in both the chair and kneeling positions. One family that tried this foot washing ritual reported arguing among the kids about who would wash whose feet. The mother told me drawing names helped resolve this problem.

4. End by gathering and reading the following prayer.

Washerwoman God[1]

Leader:
    We call you Mighty God, Father Eternal, Leader of Armies, King of Kings, Lord of Lords...

---

[1] Martha Ann Kirk. *Celebrations of Biblical Women's Stories: Tears, Milk and Honey,* "Washerwoman God" (Kansas City, Mo.: Sheed & Ward, 1987), pp. 98-100.

All: Refrain:
> But you are Washerwoman God, we know you in the waters.
> Washerwoman God, splashing, laughing, free.
> If you didn't clean the mess, where would we be?
> Scrubbing, working, sweating God, cleansing you and me.
> Make our hearts as white as snow, wash us through and
>   through.
> Washerwoman, let us be like you.

Leader:
> You put on your apron. You roll up your sleeves.
> We sought you in clouds above, while your face was here to see.

All: Refrain

Leader:
> You wash earth with brooks and streams, rivers, lakes and seas.
> Make creation fertile, bearing fruit and giving seed.

All: Refrain

Leader:
> You cleanse our face with many tears, salt that makes wounds
>   clean,
> Soaking deep and rinsing free, healing us of fear and pain.

All: Refrain

Leader:
> You kiss the shores with ocean waves, soothe hearts with gentle
>   song. Make the water teem with life, crashing free and
>   bursting strong.

All: Refrain

Leader:
> Wash the dirty diapers the baby makes with ease.
> Before we're good, while in our mess, your loving makes us free.

All: Refrain

Leader:
> You wash the air with sparkling rain, whispery drops and mist.
> Sometimes shouting torrents show your scrub board
>   cleansing fists.

All: Refrain

Leader:
> Your love brings us to table; yes, we feast on food and wine
> And you help us with the dishes after we have played and dined.

All: Refrain

Good Friday

Sooner or later most every Christian parent is questioned about why this day when Jesus died is called "Good Friday." You can explain to your children that it wasn't until after Easter that Jesus' disciples could see anything good about what happened that day. Good Friday is a reminder to us that God can bring good out of even the worst of circumstances. On this day we take time to remember Jesus' death on Calvary and to acknowledge that Jesus continues to suffer and die in our world today. Talking about Jesus' death is a good time to explain to your children that when anyone hurts, goes hungry, is lonely or is afraid, Jesus is suffering with them.

The custom of Adoration of the Cross on Good Friday dates back to the fourth century when, according to tradition, Empress Helena discovered the true cross of the crucifixion and veneration of the relic began in the Church of Jerusalem. *Veneration* is a more accurate word to describe this practice, as the adoration is reserved for Christ himself. In bowing to or kissing the cross, the faithful bend down *in body* before the cross and *in spirit* before God.

Good Friday Adoration Services are solemn and emotionally stirring. In many churches they may be too long or not otherwise appropriate for toddlers, but older children often find participation meaningful, especially if they attend year after year.

During the service the veiled crucifix is dramatically and gradually uncovered while the priest and people chant, "Behold the wood of the cross, on which hung the Savior of the world. Come let us adore." When the cross is completely unveiled, the celebrant removes his shoes, a time-honored act of reverence, approaches and kisses the cross. The faithful then follow in this sober act of worship.

If you cannot attend your parish Good Friday service you may want to hold a simple ritual at home. The cross has long been the principal symbol representing Christ's victory over death. For early Christians, however, it was primarily a reminder of a hideous form of execution. Only after the Roman Emperor Constantine banned crucifixion in the fourth century did it become a popular sign of Christianity. C.S. Lewis observed that the crucifixion did not become common in art until all those who had actually witnessed this type of death penalty had died.

Veneration of the Cross at Home

• SUGGESTED SCRIPTURE: Mark 15:22-37

You will need:
    Ten to forty minutes, depending on age of children
    Crucifix
    Several candles and matches
    Bible

A good rule of thumb for family prayer time is to plan about two minutes for every year of your child's age. Some children will have a longer attention span than others, and you'll end up compromising anyway if you have children of different ages.

1. Gather the family around the crucifix and light one or more candles. A low coffee table works well for this prayer ritual, but the kitchen table is fine.

2. Begin with the Sign of the Cross and a simple prayer asking Jesus to be with you as you set aside some quiet time to reflect on his death.

3. Read aloud the Scripture passage telling of Jesus' crucifixion.

4. After a moment of quiet, explain that Jesus' great love for each of us, his willingness to suffer and die for all people, has set us free from our sins. This is hard to understand, for children and for all of us. Though it may not make complete sense, we try to have faith in that great love. We try to model our lives on Jesus' self-giving.

5. Now invite each person to make some sign of that faith and love, perhaps by kissing or simply touching the cross. Depending on the age of your children, this can be a quick ritual or a longer quiet reflection.

6. Close by offering prayers of petition for the needs of your family, friends and the world. Use your own words or the following:

> For those who are sick or suffering (name them),
>   we pray to the Lord.
> *Lord, by your cross and Resurrection, set us free.*
> For those who are lonely or afraid, we pray to the Lord.
> *Lord, by your cross and Resurrection, set us free.*
> For those who are hungry, homeless or hopeless,
>   we pray to the Lord.
> *Lord, by your cross and Resurrection, set us free.*
> For victims of crime, war, natural disaster,
>   we pray to the Lord.
> *Lord, by your cross and Resurrection, set us free.*
> For those who have died, (name) we pray to the Lord.
> *Lord, by your cross and Resurrection, set us free.*
> *Amen.*

7. Blow out the candles and share a family hug.

HOLY SATURDAY: DAY OF WAITING

• SUGGESTED SCRIPTURE: Luke 24:13-24; Ecclesiastes 3:1-8; Micah 7:7

Coloring Easter Eggs

You will need:
    Six or more eggs
    Food coloring or egg dye
    Large coffee mugs (one for each color of dye)
    Spoons or wire egg holders

1. Place eggs in a large saucepan. Add enough water to cover the eggs. Bring to a boil on high heat, then reduce heat to a simmer and cover the pan with a lid. Cook eggs for 15 to 20 minutes. Pour off water and replace with cold water. You may add ice cubes to help cool the eggs.

2. Prepare dye for eggs according to package directions, each color in a separate mug. When the eggs are cold, drop one in a mug of dye and then remove it immediately. Ask the children why it's still white. Even little ones can probably guess. Return the egg to the dye. While the youngsters wait, perhaps stirring the egg in the cup, explain how this day is one of waiting. We wait for Jesus to rise from the dead.

3. As the children continue to color the eggs, read aloud Luke 24:13-24. Talk about how the disciples were not waiting on this day after Jesus' crucifixion. They didn't understand that Jesus would rise. What difference did the Resurrection make in the lives of the disciples? Will it make a difference in our lives? Enjoy the beauty of the colored eggs, a small symbol of the wonderful change Easter brings to our world.

3

EASTER
Discovering New Life

Alleluia! Christ is risen! Easter is the most ancient and the single most important feast day of the year for Christians. The Resurrection of Jesus is the central tenet of our faith. On this day we celebrate the Passover of Jesus from death to new life and through our baptism, our own share in the Resurrection. This includes our hope in eternal life and the spirit in which we live this earthly life. It means we live with a mindfulness that Christ is present in each person we encounter as well as those we'll never meet who live on the other side of the world. It means recognizing the Spirit is present in all creation, in every circumstance of our lives, even every breath we take. This is the gift and challenge of our inheritance as Easter people.

We celebrate Easter on a Sunday between March 22 and April 25, on the first Sunday after the first full moon after the vernal equinox. The stories, songs, customs and foods of Easter serve as symbols, which remind us of the meaning of the holiday. We don't have to pack them all in on Easter Sunday but can carry on our celebration over the next fifty days until Pentecost.

One the most popular traditions of the holiday is decorating Easter eggs. This custom stems from the time when eating eggs was forbidden during the lenten fast. Families brought eggs out in abundance on Easter day, dyed red to symbolize joy. Eggs, as well as bunny rabbits and budding flowers, are also a sign of springtime and new life. Hunting for eggs can remind us of the way in which we seek to become new creations in Christ. Dyed in rainbow colors, the eggs remind us of God's promise to Noah after the great flood. The white lily is another symbol of Easter and the Resurrection, its color a mark of purity.

The rejoicing of Easter has long been accompanied by feasting. Serving lamb on this day is a custom carried over from the Jewish

Passover at which a lamb was sacrificed and eaten. Christians understand Jesus to be the new sacrifice, the Lamb of God who, by his death, atoned for the sins of the world. Ham is another traditional Easter dish, and a sign of the new covenant in Christ whereby all foods are clean. Eating pork is forbidden by Jewish dietary law as it is considered unclean. Other Easter fare includes fresh spring vegetables and berries and sweet, rich breads, which traditionally had been given up for Lent.

These citations are given for traditional Easter Bible stories; however, for young children re-tellings in picture book form or in children's Bibles are more appropriate.

Creation: Genesis 1–2
Noah's Ark: Genesis 6:5-22; 7; 8
The Exodus: Exodus 3–15
Daniel and the Lion's Den: Daniel 6
Queen Esther: Esther 2–10
Gospel accounts of the Resurrection: Matthew 27:45–28:20;
Mark 16:42–17:11; Luke 24:1-12; John 20:1-21

EASTER TREASURE

Everybody loves discovering a hidden treasure. And it doesn't have to be a chest of gold and jewels to make our day. It can be a five-dollar bill pulled from the pocket of last year's coat, a bargain gleaned from a yard sale or a letter from a friend just when you needed it. Even simple treasures have the power to make our spirits shine.

Writer Annie Dillard tells of a game she played as a girl, hiding pennies along the sidewalk. She used chalk to draw arrows and written directions like "Surprise ahead" and "Money this way" pointing to her hidden treasures. Not staying around to watch, she only imagined the happiness people would feel upon finding her unexpected gifts.

As an adult Dillard realized the significance of treasure hunting in our everyday lives. She sees the world "studded and strewn with pennies cast broadside by a generous hand." Wherever we are and at any time there are "lots of things to see, unwrapped gifts and free surprises."

At Easter we celebrate the greatest treasure of all—the free gift, the unearned prize, the incredulous inheritance—salvation. Perhaps this treasure is too extravagant for us to readily accept. It's easier at times to focus on our unworthiness rather than on our God's generosity, easier to believe in judgment than in mercy and love.

A treasure hunt will do wonders. Waking each day ready to see the marvels that surround us will gradually open our hearts to the most astounding mystery of all.

I like to place a vase of fresh flowers on my desk. Even the simplest bloom, like a daffodil or daisy, never ceases to amaze me. The vibrant colors and the delicate textures feed my hungry soul. Taking a moment from my work to appreciate their beauty fills me with awe and admiration for the Creator. It helps train me to notice the world around me with more gratitude. And little by little, as I get in the habit of hunting treasures, I get out of the habit of feeling deprived, anxious and cynical. Beginning to appreciate the many pennies strewn by a generous hand has led to greater faith in the boundless love that led Jesus to give his life for me.

Easter Treasure Hunt for Children

You will need:

Thirty minutes to one hour

A cross: symbol of Christ's redeeming death.

A rock: symbol of the empty tomb.

A scrap of cloth: symbol of the cloth that had wrapped Jesus' body, that the women found when they discovered the empty tomb.

A piece of bread: symbol of the bread Christ changed into his body.

A cluster of grapes: symbol of the wine Christ changed into his blood.

A flower: symbol of life Jesus promises those who love him.

A candle: symbol of Jesus' love, the light of the world.

1. Gather the children and remind them of the Easter story. Perhaps they have just heard it at Mass. If not, you may want to read them a passage from a children's Bible or an appropriate storybook.

2. Ask them to guess the significance of each of the objects listed. You may ask older children to look through the Bible for a verse that applies to each symbol. If they need a hint, refer them to one of the Gospel accounts of Jesus' Passion.

3. Send the children to another room while you hide the items.

4. Call them back in and begin the treasure hunt. As the objects are found, arrange them on the table or a shelf. Throughout the Easter season light the candle and use the symbols as a source or starting point for prayer.

Easter Season Morning Prayer

Mark the days of the Easter season by gathering your family each morning for prayer. You may want to use this one, which is based on Psalm 118:

> This is the day that God has made; let us rejoice and be glad.
> Let us give thanks for God is good, and God's love endures forever.
> We have no fear for God is with us. The Risen Christ is our Savior.
> This is the day that God has made; let us rejoice and be glad.

CELEBRATING EASTER EVERY DAY

When the Easter eggs are gone, the holiday may begin to slip from our minds. As our secular culture moves on to whatever new and improved fad comes next, it's our challenge as Christian parents to keep the spirit of Easter alive and thriving in our families.

My grade school son seemed surprised when I told him that Easter was the most important day of the year. "Isn't Christmas more important?" he asked. I explained that Jesus' Resurrection was the central point of our faith, but ideas like the paschal mystery can be hard for kids to understand.

Concrete examples and stories from everyday life can bring the meaning of Easter alive for children. It can also help them to see that Easter is not just a holiday that comes once a year, but a way of seeing that defines the way we live every day.

Here are a few ways you can help communicate the Easter experience of new life to your children.

1. Share and listen.

Teach faith with a well-chosen word here and there and an ear tuned to the truth of your child's experience. Exploring the reality of Easter with young children can be as simple as pointing out how God's power heals a child's scratch, cut or broken bone.

Talk with your children about how the same power of God that raised Jesus from death is available to free us from our bad habits, our worries and our problems. Take a moment to explain that Christ's life is present in your family and how sharing your troubles with others can help lessen the burden. Suggest how family members can encourage and support each other as they try to overcome bad habits.

We don't have to wait for heaven to experience new life and the joy of resurrection. Ask your children if they can think of examples.

Perhaps share with your children how daily prayer strengthens your faith. Ask them what strategies they use when they feel overwhelmed by chores or homework. Tell stories of hard times in the past and how God stayed faithful to your family and helped you come through struggles.

2. Plant seeds.

Here's an easy way to see new life grow. You'll need a plate, a washcloth and seeds. Choose seeds that are not too tiny and germinate quickly like nasturtium, morning glory, cucumber or pumpkin. Dampen the washcloth and lay it on the plate. Evenly space seeds over half of the washcloth. Fold the other half over on top of the seeds and place in a sunny window.

Explain to your child that seeds appear after a plant flowers and dies back. Left on its own, it would fall to the ground and die, allowing a new plant to grow from it. Have older children look up and read John 12:24.

Your child can peek at the seeds every day. Keep the cloth damp, but not soggy. Within seven to ten days, the seeds should sprout and begin to grow roots. When the roots are about half an inch long, plant the sprouts into pots of soil or outside.

3. Take a nature walk.

A simple walk down the road or around the block offers a multitude of opportunities to appreciate God's handiwork. In rural areas trees and flowers will be budding or blooming during the Easter season.

In the city children will be able to spot a valiant weed or grass perhaps springing up through a crack in the pavement. God's life is present in the people or animals we might see, in the breeze against our cheek, in the colors of the sky. Let a toddler set her own pace on a nature walk and point out to you what catches her eye. You might ask older children to remain quiet on the walk in order to be attentive to their senses.

4. Hatch a chick.

This project requires more time, expense and commitment, but watching a chick hatch from an egg is truly an unforgettable experience for children. It's a powerful demonstration of new life coming forth. Contact your local farm supply store for fertilized eggs, incubators and instructions. Children enjoy feeding, watching and petting a fluffy chick. Be sure to have a good home lined up if you cannot accommodate a full-grown chicken.

An alternative is to arrange a visit to a local farm to observe chicks hatching or newborn calves or lambs with their mothers. These types of experiences, once common for most children and now rare for suburban and city families, help bring home the mystery of new life and inspire a sense of awe and wonder in our youngsters.

These are just a few of the myriad ways that we can acknowledge the power of new life in our lives and help our children see Easter in every day.

Easter Freedom

As a teenager, Bridget had such poor eyesight that if a friend stood two feet in front of her she often could not see clearly enough to recognize her face. Although glasses improved her vision, Bridget rarely wore them. They were as thick as Coke bottles and she hated them. "I didn't feel like a geek, but I knew I looked like one," she says.

Bridget's vision problems made communication difficult. Since she couldn't see people's facial expressions as they spoke, she lost some of the meaning or tone of the conversation. When she cracked a joke, she couldn't tell whether people were smiling or looking confused. Even when Bridget wore her glasses so she could see, she felt shy and lacked confidence. This vision impairment robbed Bridget of the freedom to be her true self.

Then, at age twenty-one, Bridget had radial keratotomy surgery that restored her to almost perfect vision. "It felt like a miracle, a turning point in my life," she says. Clear eyesight gave her a new sense of freedom to be the person she always imagined she could be.

Isn't it just what each of us longs for? We know that Christ offers perfect freedom as Paul wrote to the Romans (6:4) "...Just as Christ was raised from the dead by the glory of the Father, we too might walk in newness of life." Sometimes, though, this fundamental truth is difficult to grasp. We can be trapped by minor tyrannies in our day-to-day life, and not be able to live with the freedom that is our baptismal right.

An insidious tyrant I found running loose in my house was my desire to be a "good mother." Without realizing it, I sometimes confuse being a good mother with making my children happy. The tyranny became clear at the end of a long day when I went to my room, shut the door and gave in to tears. I had withstood several hours of nagging by my five-year-old before finally making a special trip to the store so he could spend his five dollars, hot from Grandma and burning a hole in his pocket. An hour later I found myself trying to placate him as he pitched a fit because his new toy disappointed his expectations. His older sister and brother further stretched my nerves by taunting him, and I ended up arguing with my husband while trying to "fix" my son's hurt and disappointed feelings. I had been sucked into the big lie that I was responsible for my child's happiness and had become a slave in the process.

Being a good mother does not mean keeping my children happy. Knowing that frees me to help them live through the pain and disappointment that is sure to come in their lives. And it frees me to face the pain and disappointment present in my own life, allowing me to stop doing and fixing, stressing and stewing. I am able to just be.

The freedom we discover in our everyday lives as we journey in relationship with God may not be the vivid experience of Bridget, going from myopia to clear sight. But small bursts of freedom building upon one another in our lives are proof of the new life Jesus promised.

PENTECOST: A POWERFUL WIND

Some passages of Scripture read with all the drama of a tale told around the campfire. The story of Pentecost is one of them.

> When the day of Pentecost had come, they were all together in one place. And suddenly from heaven there came a sound like the rush of a violent wind, and it filled the entire house where they were sitting. Divided tongues, as of fire, appeared among them, and a tongue rested on each of them. All of them were filled with the Holy Spirit.... (Acts: 2:1-4)

Perhaps in hearing this reading year after year, we lose some of the drama. Our lives seem so far removed from biblical times, and it's sometimes difficult to be aware of the power of God in the here and now. At Pentecost the power of the Holy Spirit filled Christ's disciples and empowered them, not only to go out and preach the Good News but also to give their lives for their faith. How does this relate to work at the office, to cooking and laundry, to driving kids to soccer or baseball and to the end of the school year time crunch?

It is the indwelling of the Spirit that empowers people to act for justice, to make life-giving choices and to discover voices with which to preach the Good News. This power is available to us, just as it was to those first disciples.

This Pentecost, let's follow their example. Let's gather together and listen for the sound of a violent wind. Let's open our lives to make room for the power of the Spirit. Through our baptism we have been empowered to bring the Good News of justice to our homes, our workplaces and our world.

My family began asking questions in the car on the way to Mass on Pentecost Sunday. I didn't have all the answers, so I did a little research. It pays to be ready. Any minute a child could start asking you the following questions:

1. *Why do we wear red today?*
  The church has designated symbolic colors to mark the different seasons and some feast days of the liturgical year. You'll see the priest dressed in these colored vestments, as well as possibly draperies in the church or tablecloths or candles in people's homes. The red of Pentecost symbolizes the fire of the Holy Spirit that came upon Jesus' disciples in the Upper Room at the first Pentecost.

2. *Why didn't the tongues of flame catch the disciple's heads on fire?*
Think of Moses and the burning bush that was not consumed. With
God, all things are possible. If this answer doesn't satisfy, you may
go on to explain how Catholics don't necessarily take the Bible word
for word. Some stories are metaphorical, meaning the words imply
a truth too big or mysterious to completely understand. The power
of the Holy Spirit can be seen in how the disciples became filled
with the courage to go out and live and preach the Good News, but
it cannot be completely defined. Imagining the disciples on fire with
God's love is one way of trying to describe this power.

3. *What does* Pentecost *mean anyway?*
Pentecost is a Greek word for fiftieth, and came from the Jewish
spring harvest festival, which was celebrated on the fiftieth day after
Passover. The Israelites marked the end of the wheat and barley
harvest at this feast and brought their first fruits to the temple as
offerings to God. In the time of Jesus, Pentecost had also become a
celebration of the giving of the covenant law to Moses. The
Christian feast of Pentecost celebrates the gift of the Spirit as the
first fruits of our inheritance as children of God, as well as the new
covenant we have in Christ.

4. *What is the Holy Spirit?*
In the Hebrew experience and Scriptures the Spirit is the life-giving
breath of God, which comes upon a person, renewing her from
within and making her responsive to God's Word. Before Jesus'
Ascension he promised to send the Spirit, which would make his
teachings clear to his followers and give them the courage and wisdom to continue his work.

The church defines the Holy Spirit as the third person of the
Trinity, the power that enables faith and unites us to God and each
other.

5. *Is the Spirit still around today?*
The Spirit of God takes no vacations. Looking around we see division and discord in the Body of Christ. We're not only separated into
different Christian denominations, but the Catholic church itself is
divided by scandal and polarized into conservative and liberal
camps.

Even so, the Spirit is at work with each step we take toward reconciliation. When we choose to listen to one another and believe the other is acting in good faith—that is the Spirit. When we refrain from quick, easy answers and accept a life with tension—that is the Spirit. When we are willing to risk our deepest fears and share our pain—that is the Spirit. When we stop trying to convince others that we're right and begin to search for mutual understanding—that is the Spirit.

I also like to think the Spirit is at work as I struggle for answers when my kids ask me questions.

LIFE LESSONS FROM THE GARDEN

I dragged myself out to the garden a month later than usual this spring. In fact, I almost didn't put in a garden at all, but I'm glad I made the effort. Lessons learned in gardening apply equally to family relationships and my writing life.

Just one afternoon of working the soil and a deep knowing touched me like a gentle breeze—a knowing that knocked me into the big, soft, grandmother lap of God. I sank, comfortable and comforted, reflecting on my need to let go and allow the Creator a freer hand.

The truth that dawns as I dig in the dirt comes from so deep it must flow in my blood. My sowing and harvesting is modest. But I'm descended from a long line of farmers stretching from the Depression years in the Midwest to the early settling of the fertile river valleys of the eastern United States and for countless generations in Western Europe. Family members before me depended on their planting and growing efforts for their very survival. I merely nurture several pots of tomatoes, a few hills of beans and squash, basil, some perennial herbs and a few blooming plants for show around my front porch.

Yet this spring even a small garden seemed too much. In the middle of writing assignments, end-of-school projects and the kids in baseball, I felt too overwhelmed to even think of gardening. In the late afternoon I scraped up just enough energy to agonize over what to cook for dinner and how to catch up on the housework.

After days of this, I traded the cool house for the bright sunshine and my garden tools. My few hours of hard work paid off with more than potted vegetables and bright colored blossoms. I sprouted a new attitude too.

Gardening requires diligent work: preparing the earth, planting seeds, nursing young plants, watering and fertilizing. Then there's a point where the gardener lets go and waits, knowing God must do the rest. No amount of effort will make the plants grow, bloom and produce. The touch of the Almighty brings forth the fruit, or not.

One may pull a few weeds, stake a few vines—and pinch off extraneous shoots. Those tasks—sometimes deliberate, sometimes haphazard—are done, however, with the recognition that the gardener is cocreator. There's no sense of urgent responsibility, no driven anxiety, but rather a wisdom that the growing continues outside the gardener's control.

This picture, so clear when applied to the garden, muddles in the midst of real life as a mother and writer working at home.

Often as a parent I've been impatient with my children. Why don't they pick up their books and toys, put their dirty laundry in the hamper, do their chores? It seems I've told them a thousand times. And yet as I pause this week to consider my oldest son as he graduates from eighth grade, I notice things I hadn't before. His books stand organized by subject on their shelves. He now sorts his laundry and operates the washer and dryer with ease. It's been three or four years since I've needed to remind him to do his homework or practice his saxophone.

I realize I could have tended my son's growth with much less worry, frustration and impatience. I could nurture family life with more of a spirit of calm, waiting for the buds to unfold. I could torture myself less about my writing and free the creativity within.

And so a long, put-off afternoon of gardening became a reminder of how I am cocreator with the Creator, an invitation to trust that my efforts are enough, that I am not totally responsible for the outcome of my labor. I'm reminded of the words of the late Archbishop of San Salvador, Oscar Romero. "We are workers, not master builders; ministers, not messiahs. We are prophets of a future that is not our own."

4

ORDINARY TIME
Moments of Grace

The weeks that fall between the church seasons are called Ordinary Time. There are two blocks of Ordinary Time, one in winter after Christmas and before Lent, and another in summer and fall beginning after Easter Time and ending at Advent. But Ordinary Time has taken on the connotation of *everyday* meaning *customary* or nothing special. Together they take up over half the year, over half of our lives. Ordinary, maybe, but important all the same.

Most of us sometimes yearn to escape the ordinariness of our lives. We may enjoy a passing fantasy about winning the lottery; more often we may ache for our lives to have deeper meaning. We long to be holy, or at least good, boldly like the martyrs of old, or in a quiet, Mother Teresa style. It's not always clear to us that our stumbling attempts to follow God's call faithfully, amid the demanding routine of family life, do require holiness.

Faithful Christian living requires qualities like courage, persistence, vision, self-giving love and fidelity. These are the qualities of great saints. Yet, it is in our ordinary days as Christians that we practice these virtues and fulfill God's purpose for our lives. In the midst of what may seem to the world to be our anonymous, unimportant days, we grow in loving relationship with God, others and ourselves. Within these relationships we make our contribution to bringing about God's kingdom.

Rituals are one way of recognizing the holy in our ordinary lives. High rituals like baptisms, graduations and weddings mark big moments of change. Everyday rituals like bedtime stories or a cup of morning coffee mark our routine passages. A ritual can be any conscious action that expresses a deeper meaning. Humans have practiced them since time began and often we do them without noticing. We can deliberately choose to include rituals in our family life to nurture, heal and celebrate.

As Catholics we experience the transforming power of ritual through Eucharist. Each Mass we gather to break bread just as Christians have done since the Last Supper the night before Jesus died. This action, though repeated again and again, is always new. It changes us from our individual sinful selves to the Body of Christ alive in the world. Simple, small rituals practiced in the midst of our sometimes hectic family schedules have a similar ability to open our lives and let the presence of God shine through.

This chapter is organized to reflect some of the ups and downs of ordinary family life and suggests rituals, activities and thoughts to ponder. Whether it is *mealtime, holiday time, summertime, prayer time, discipline time* or *crisis time,* we recognize God is present.

MEALTIME

• SUGGESTED SCRIPTURE: Mark 1:34-43; 14:22; Proverbs 15:17; 17:1

The traditional mealtime where the whole family gathers and sits down at the table to eat home-cooked food has become countercultural. In the United States, 50 percent of all meals consumed are fast food. And even the drive through is becoming too slow. Diners in a hurry can now buy the world's simplest sandwich, a Smuckers PB&J®, ready to eat with the crusts already cut off. Or for breakfast there are Milk'nCereal bars with Cheerios® on the outside and real milk filling. Teenagers say they find it inconvenient to eat an apple or peel an orange. Our busy, fast-paced lives make big profits for companies selling single-serving nutritional drinks. These one-handed meals are perfect for on-the-go eating, but do meals like this feed our bodies at the expense of our souls?

In many parishes when children prepare to receive First Eucharist, parents are reminded that the experience of family mealtimes is primary in a child's understanding of the sacrament. If this is true, what is fast food teaching our children?

This question burst into public debate in Europe when Italian theologian Father Massimo Salani published a book on the topic of how faith and food are related. He questioned the "heavenliness" of fast food, saying that eating quickly and alone is the antithesis of receiving Eucharist, which we do together in celebration as a community. Father Salani went so far as to say fast food "is not Catholic. It completely forgets the holiness of food."

His pronouncements drew disapproval faster than a teenager smashing a packet of ketchup in a crowded booth. The Italian newspaper *Il Messagero* proclaimed the "excommunication of the hamburger." And McDonald's Italia wasted no time in assuring the public a Big Mac and fries are compatible with the world's faiths.

Father Salani is not the only voice rising to protest fast food. Slow Food, an international movement started in Italy and spreading around the world, endeavors to revive the pleasures and benefits of savoring rather than scarfing. Slow Food devotees seek to enjoy the flavor, freshness and texture of food. They delight in sharing meals and in the knowledge of where and how food is produced.

One Slow Food project helps farmers in Nicaragua recover agricultural land, another saves fruits and vegetables at risk of extinction, and another promotes regional cuisine in danger of dying as our tastes become homogenized. But the movement primarily persuades people to sit down together, relax and savor each other's company and every bite they eat.

I must admit dinnertime is not perfect at the Farrell house. Sometimes cross words are spoken; sometimes food flies. Manners are...well, improving. But we're all in the same room together, and we're paying attention. You may have to wait to speak, or shout, but you will get heard. The children may argue over who leads the blessing, but at least they're praying.

Just as the menu feeds our body's need for nutrients, the gathering and spending time together on a daily basis nourishes our spirits and family bonds. Most parents love their children. One couple told me they *like* theirs, and they learned to like them at dinner.

A mother of six says mealtimes together taught them to listen. She says, "We involve each person, from youngest to oldest, and try to give our heartfelt attention to details from the teen's volleyball game to the preschooler's latest art project. We discuss hard issues too: politics, racism in our town, friends who are unexpectedly pregnant, using drugs or losing a parent to cancer. Lots of life happens over spaghetti."

Can families relax, listen to one another, resolve disputes and voice affection and appreciation over fast food? Certainly. But to cultivate the kind of relationships modeled by Christ and celebrated in the

Eucharist takes time—time that is difficult to come by in our fast-food culture.

It may be impossible for a family in our society to completely swear off fast food. Slow Food may be too much of a stretch as well. But here are some suggestions for adding a bit of holiness to the everyday business of eating:

1. Try to gather all the family for at least one meal a day.

2. Include your children in preparing the food.

3. Turn off TV and radio, and put away newspapers before eating.

4. Pray before meals. Converse during them.

5. Practice slow eating by taking a sip of water or laying down your fork between every few bites.

6. Invite someone who's alone to share a family meal.

7. Taste a fruit or vegetable you've never eaten before.

8. Bake bread from scratch.

9. Notice the nutritional content of whole foods versus processed foods.

10. Visit a farm to remind yourself where food comes from.

Traditional Catholic Grace Before Meals

Bless us, O Lord, and these Thy gifts, which we about to receive from Thy bounty through Christ Our Lord, Amen.

Open, Shut Them: Grace for Young Children

Open, Shut them (Hold up hands with open palms facing outward. Close fingers into a fist as you say "shut them.")

Open, shut them (Repeat as above.)

Give a little clap. (Clap)

Open, shut them (Repeat open and shutting motions with fingers.)
Open, shut them (Repeat.)
Fold them in your lap. (Fold hands for prayer.)

Sing the following to the tune of "Yankee Doodle."

We give you thanks for happy hearts for rain and sunny weather.
We thank you for the food we eat and that we are together.

Superman Grace

Sing to the tune and arm motions of "Superman" TV show theme song.

Thank you Lord, for giving us food.
Thank you Lord, for giving us food.
For the food we eat, for the friends we meet,
Thank you Lord, for being so good.

"Rock Around the Clock" Grace

Sing to the tune of "Rock Around the Clock."

God is great. God is good. Let us thank him for our food.
Gonna thank him in the morning, gonna thank him at night.

Simple Grace

Sing to the tune of "Frére Jacques."

God our Father, God our Mother, once again, once again.
We would like to thank you; we would like to thank you.
Amen. Amen.

Johnny Appleseed Grace

O, the Lord is good to me, and so I thank the Lord,
For giving me the things I need, the sun and the rain and the apple
seed.

O, the Lord is good to me.
Amen. Amen.

Traditional Grace

Thank you for the world so sweet,
Thank you for the food we eat.
Thank you for the birds that sing,
Thank you, God, for everything.
Amen.

CELEBRATING SPECIAL DAYS

- SUGGESTED SCRIPTURE: Psalm 8:2-10; 126:2-3; 139:13-17; 148:1-14;
  Matthew 5:14-16; 1 Corinthians 1:31
  2 Timothy 4:7

You probably already have ways of celebrating special days like birthdays and anniversaries. It's not difficult to add a spiritual dimension to your festivities. The ideas and prayers to follow can be used on a child's birthday or to celebrate many different events or milestones such as the anniversary of a child's baptism, participation in sports or music, leaving for a trip or summer camp or to celebrate accomplishments or a good effort. You need not have an elaborate ceremony. Simply taking time to read a short Scripture passage before a meal, or to lay your hand on a child in blessing is enough.

Blessing of a Child

Some parents make a habit of blessing their children each day. Any time is OK for the blessing, but you probably want to choose a time when the child is not distracted or busy with something else. Some good times are before a meal, before a child leaves for school or play or at bedtime.

Say, "I'd like to bless you now." Then lay your hand on your child's head and speak the blessing. You may use your own words, the Sign of the Cross or the following, an ancient blessing based on Psalm 67, "May the Lord bless you and keep you. May the Lord shine his face upon you, be gracious to you and give you peace."

Prayer to Honor a Person on a Special Day

Sung to the tune of "Frére Jacques."
> (Name) is special. (Name) is special. God made her so. God made her so.
> No wonder that we love her. No wonder that we love her.
> Thank you, God. Thank you, God.

NATIONAL HOLIDAYS

• SUGGESTED SCRIPTURE: Psalm 37:3; Luke 4:18-19; John 1:1-5

National holidays like Memorial Day, Fourth of July, Veterans' Day and others each have their own traditions and rituals. Without taking away from those we can add a spiritual dimension to help our families celebrate more fully. This can be as simple as beginning the day with a family prayer, Scripture reading, or song focused on the holiday. These can help our children learn to put national pride in context with religious faith.

Prayer for National Holidays

> Thank you, God, for our country and all the gifts of our land and our people. Thank you for the freedoms we enjoy and for those over the centuries who have sacrificed for those freedoms. Fill us with your spirit so that we might be wise and courageous in fulfilling our responsibilities as citizens. Help us to be generous in contributing our gifts for the common good. Bless our efforts to do your will. Amen.

Suggested Songs:
"America," lyrics by Samuel F. Smith, (1808-1895), music by *Thesaurus Musicaus* (1744)
"This is my Song," lyrics by Lloyd Stone, ©1934, ©1962, music by Jean Sibelius, (1865-1957)

SUMMERTIME

I counted the days until school let out. Now, just a week into summer vacation, I'm ready to send my kids back. With the lack of routine and constant interruptions, I can't seem to get anything accomplished.

Finishing breakfast at 10 A.M., I finally settle down to work and the disturbances begin. "Can I go play at Rory's house? When is my turn on the computer? I can't find my bicycle helmet. The ice cream man is coming! Please...please...can we have ice cream?"

Not that I don't love my children, but it is an adjustment having them home all day. They can really foul up my to-do list.

Yesterday my whole afternoon schedule was thrown off when my eight-year-old suffered a concussion. He and the neighbor boys were playing a game where they got inside sleeping bags and stumbled around tackling each other. My son fell, hit his head and was out cold. I spent the rest of the day sitting with him offering aid and comfort and keeping him awake in order to monitor his mental state.

It gave me plenty of time to think, and I realized my own mental state could use some monitoring. Somehow I'd latched onto unrealistic expectations for the summer.

I'd pictured myself working away at my writing six hours a day, keeping up with my exercise regimen and daily prayer practice, tending my vegetable garden, visiting the library, taking family hikes and bike rides, picnicking with friends and going camping. All that on top of the usual cooking and laundry and spending time with my husband and children. Then in my spare time I'd relax on the porch with a friend and a pitcher of lemonade.

Even barring Dylan's unexpected knock on the head, it would be impossible to expand summer days to fit such a schedule. I should have remembered that from last summer.

What had begun to feel like chaos and overwhelming frustration this first week the kids were out of school became manageable, a source of grace even, when I revised my expectations.

That revision came about through a change in focus, a seeking of fruitfulness rather than achievement. These two words may conjure up various images, but in the sense I mean, achievement is most often measured in dollars and cents, control and power or recognition and results. Fruitfulness, on the other hand, is not so easily gauged. Its measure may be intangible, the outcome invisible.

Achievement for me might be five pages written, kitchen cleaned, children neither bored nor bickering and dinner in the oven. Fruitfulness, however, would more likely stem from spending the afternoon being present to a sick and scared child.

The difference between the two is not always apparent on the surface. Most of us have work to do, tasks to accomplish. The question is how to bear fruit, rather than just crossing off another item from our list of things to do.

Perhaps it is the spirit with which we approach our work that becomes important. A good clue for me is how I feel.

Achievement feels tense to me, a clinging to control or a drive for perfection. It's like I have this motor running inside, revving up and not about to stop for anything until the goal is reached.

Fruitfulness feels flowing, like letting go. It's writing five pages with no need to count them. Success is less important than faithfulness, acceptance of flaws, trust and surrender. Jesus models fruitfulness for us.

With this in mind I'm ready for the rest of the summer. If I get too attached to my to-do list again, please God, no more injured children. A little nudge should be enough.

Keep Holy the Summer

For some families all routine seems to go out the open windows during summer vacation. If you're not careful, spiritual life will take a holiday too.

Here are some suggestions for remembering the Eleventh Commandment—Keep Holy the Summer:

1. *Cultivate a sense of gratitude.*
   Greet each child with a smile in the morning, thanking God aloud for the gift that a child is. Summer offers innumerable examples of the glory and abundance of God's creative genius. From a sprouting seed to the beauty of full bloom, model for your children appreciation of God's gifts.

2. *Rededicate yourselves to mealtime prayer.*
   Whether it's a picnic at the park or hotdogs on the run, begin with bowed heads and thanksgiving. Light a candle. A citronella can do double duty—God is present; bugs aren't! A simple ritual like holding hands, saying "Thank you, God," together and blowing out the candle can be a graced moment for your family.

3. *Commit to Sunday Mass even when traveling or camping.*
   This speaks powerfully to your children about the centrality of your faith. Sunday best dress isn't always necessary.

4. *Extend your family circle.*
   Whether it's the new child on the block or the elderly neighbor you don't see all winter, summer is the perfect time to reach out and include them. Don't fuss about making special plans; just invite others to join whatever you're already doing.

5. Serve others.

Teens can mow lawns; grade-schoolers can walk dogs or pick up mail. Kids are often more than willing to do chores for someone else than to do them at home. Volunteer service works wonders for boredom. Older teens may even be able to volunteer for a week away from home in programs helping disadvantaged children or underprivileged communities.

6. Don't forget Vacation Bible School (VBS) for younger children.

VBS curriculums teach faith lessons in creative, fun and kid-centered ways. They are also great opportunities for both children and parents to make new friends.

If this list sounds like a six-point plan for stressing out your summer—relax. Spirituality is a journey taken one step at a time. You never know—some of these ideas may become habits you'll carry into the school year next fall.

Thank God for Water!

There is nothing more refreshing on a hot summer day than cool water. Water is one of those blessings we often take for granted, whether it's a shower in the morning, a way to keep our lawn green, or a place to water-ski on vacation. Not every kid in America has access to a swimming pool, but in most homes you can turn on a faucet and water comes out—cool, clear water that's fit to drink.

An important part of living a Christian life is recognizing and appreciating the gifts we've been given. Water is a precious gift necessary to sustain life. In baptism it is the symbol of our new life in the Body of Christ. Water is an aid to cleanliness. It's used to produce electricity to power machinery, bring light in the darkness and heat in the cold. People and goods are transported great distances on rivers and oceans. Water offers uncountable ways of recreation and celebration.

Summer is a great time to acknowledge and be grateful for the many blessings of water. Look for ways to celebrate and give thanks, or follow some of these suggestions:

1. When washing or bathing your child make the sign of the cross on her forehead and remind her that she was baptized into the Christian family with water.

2. While your children play in the sprinkler or battle with super-soakers ask them to pause for a moment, hold hands and briefly thank God for the gift of water and the fun it provides.

3. On car trips identify lakes, rivers or streams you pass. Make an unplanned stop and have the whole family hop out and wiggle their toes in the water for just five minutes.

4. Check the library for a book of science experiments. Find some using water that are age appropriate for your children. Spend an afternoon doing hands-on learning.

5. For one day be conscious of each time you use water, and be grateful. Plan a quiet prayer time next to a fountain, bubbling stream, duck pond or fishbowl. Look, listen and give thanks.

6. Ask your family to help come up with ways to conserve and respect water. If the kids volunteer to cut back on taking baths, accept the suggestion in good fun and help keep the discussion enjoyable. Focus on the idea of how we take care of a special gift given to us by someone we love. Children can turn off the water while brushing their teeth. Teenagers can read labels on products used in the home to determine if any contain chemicals that contribute to water pollution. Parents might install water-saving showerheads or consider landscaping part (or the entire yard) with native plants and grasses which do not require watering.

In the beginning, according to Genesis, there was water. With our stewardship this gift will continue to sustain life, provide recreation and lend power for generations to come.

DISCIPLINE TIME

• SUGGESTED SCRIPTURE: Proverbs 14:26; 15:1; 22:6; Matthew 6:25-27

Most parents spend a good part of their time problem solving, disciplining or just plain pulling their hair out. We need God's faithful presence at these times. I wish I could say that I remembered each morning to ask God to help me be a good parent. So often, it is after I've lost my calm, after I've made a poor decision, that I realize my need for God.

I remember when I was a child, one of my relatives had a copy of the Morning Offering stuck on the corner of her bathroom mirror. It remained there for decades, though it was faded with age, and I'm sure she had the words memorized. I realize now that it was a reminder for her to start each day by coming into the presence of God. We could start each day with a prayer asking God to guide us through the joys and challenges of parenting.

Parent's Prayer

O God, who is Father and Mother of us all,

Guide me in this great work of parenting.

I can't do everything. I can't be perfect. Help me to do what I can, the best I can, and to have faith that you can bring good even from my mistakes.

Teach me to love unconditionally, to forgive and to seek forgiveness.

Help me to be firm and steady, kind and gentle in disciplining my children. Give me a sense of humor and a view to the long term. May I listen well, and speak with care.

Grant me the grace to grow and learn and to know when to seek the help of others.

Fill me with your spirit of strength when I am tired, hope when I despair and trust when I am tempted to give in to fear.

Bless me with the wisdom to build a joyous, peaceful and loving home in which your spirit will always abide. Amen.

Firm and Kind

Thank God I've never been caught by a security camera while disciplining my children. I have resolved never to hit my kids, but who knows how I might look to strangers when I've lost my temper. Maybe like a wild-eyed, yelling, threatening crazy woman who just might do anything?

High Christian ideals have the potential to cause us to expect too much of our children, overreact to their shortcomings and come down too hard on them. When we hear about the dangers of teenage sex, violence, drug and alcohol use and cheating in schools, we can let our fear get the better of us. We risk heavy-handedness when we send our three-year-old to his room with no dinner for refusing to share; harangue our adolescent until she bursts into tears; insist our teenager does it our way, because "I said so."

I remember when my oldest was two, and refusing to be buckled into his car seat. "If I can't get him to obey me now," I thought, "whatever will I do when he's fifteen." I picked him up and thrust him in. He bawled, but I held him down until he stopped struggling, and I could manage to buckle him tight.

For several years I took his attempts at independence personally. I'm a slow learner, but eventually I realized if kids did everything perfect the first time, they wouldn't need parents. For example, if adolescents aren't pushing the limits, they're not doing the work of a particular developmental stage. Like when they were two, early teens are striving for more autonomy, but also wanting to know the boundaries that keep them safe.

In the heat of the moment, we parents may also forget that certain skills come with time and experience, such as how to make a truly heartfelt apology, with no excuses, no blaming. I catch my elementary-age youngsters in the middle of an emotional battle, and I expect them to work it out flawlessly.

The heavy responsibility of raising Christian children can blind me to the power of mercy and love. Fear of not disciplining enough can drive me to correct my child too severely.

Franciscan friar Richard Rohr says it this way:

> You cannot give yourself away until you have a self. That's why the gospel was meant primarily for adults. The most we can do with children is love them and touch them; cuddle, hug and believe in them. You can't preach a full-fledged, heavy gospel to children because everything in their psyche and soul is saying grow, experience, develop, run, prove myself, be ambitious. A child's psyche cannot understand the way of the cross.[2]

There is also another side to the equation. We can be too permissive with our children. We can be so concerned with praising them and

---

[2] Rohr, Richard. *Radical Grace: Daily Meditations* by Richard Rohr. John Feister, ed., (Cincinnati: St. Anthony Messenger Press, 1995), p. 332.

making sure their needs are met that they develop a sense of entitlement. We can be so busy and stressed we don't have the energy to discipline. We may find it easier to give material things than to spend time together as a family.

I sometimes struggle with allowing my youngest son to experience the negative consequences of his behavior. He has a habit of pitching a fit when he doesn't get his way. As a family we've agreed on consequences for throwing a tantrum, being disrespectful or shouting at others. But I've found myself not following through because I'm tired, trying to get dinner on the table and feeling sorry for him because I know he's had a rough day. Or I don't ask him to do a chore because I know it'll provoke a scene, and I just don't have the energy to deal with it.

This type of parenting is not good for my child. It encourages him to be irresponsible and reinforces the idea that he need not be concerned about others.

Raising our children requires both discipline and love. Each day can bring new challenges to our hearts and our skills. It's impossible to do a perfect job of walking the fine line that joins correction and affection. Keeping in mind they are two halves of the whole, we can continue striving to balance firmness and kindness.

A Call from the Principal's Office

There's nothing like a call from the principal's office to send a parent's heart racing into high gear. I've never known such a call to bring good news.

I breathe again when I hear no bones were broken and no ambulance called. But my stomach knots as I wonder how my child might have misbehaved.

This time the call from the principal's office turned into a powerful lesson in parenting, and gave me a deeper understanding of God's merciful love. What began as bad news actually became a blessing.

My third-grader had been sent to the principal's office for misbehavior and assigned lunch-hour detention the following day.

"He's a wonderful boy," said the principal. "But I wanted you to know."

"Thank you," I said. "I appreciate your call."

I knew this particular child would feel terrible about what had happened. The punishment at school would be more than enough. He came home that day with his head low and a face about to crumble. I pulled him onto my lap and gathered him into a hug. It didn't take long for the whole story to come pouring out.

"It's OK," I told him. "I love you."

I didn't feel the need to lecture or discipline. It was clear he had learned his lesson and all he needed was love. The consequences of his actions had dispensed more wisdom than I could offer. It felt good just to hold him tightly.

It reminded me of a story a friend once told me about the day she skipped junior high and ended up getting arrested for smoking marijuana. She still cringes remembering how she had to call her parents from the police station to come and pick her up. They didn't say a word. She waited all afternoon and through dinner for some dire punishment. None came. That evening her father carried through on plans to take her ballroom dancing, something they often did together.

The incident made a strong impression on this young woman. She never skipped school again, and now, some thirty years later, she still speaks about that special night and the love she felt from her father.

Why do I sometimes think that in order to make my children do better, they must first feel worse? When I make a mistake, God doesn't smite me down. Yes, sometimes I do feel terrible when I've done something wrong, but God is waiting with open arms ready to forgive me. The knowledge of God's loving mercy gives me the courage to face my own sinfulness. Without faith in God's unconditional love it would be hard to admit my guilt, hard to find the strength to try to do better next time.

One dad told me about the Sunday his teenage son came back from Communion and plowed into his younger brother who happened to be blocking his way into the pew.

"I was steaming," said the dad. "I wanted to grab him and shake him, give him a stern lecture. But we were in church. I couldn't do a thing."

Later in the day his anger diminished and he took his son aside. In a calm voice he told the teenager that he had seen what had happened, and that he hoped never to see such behavior again. To his surprise, the boy admitted he shouldn't have shoved his younger brother and agreed he wouldn't do it again.

"I was used to him arguing whenever things like this happened. This time I wasn't angry and accusing, so he wasn't defensive. I pointed out his behavior, and I was loving. I think that allowed him to admit he'd done wrong and wanted to do better."

I hope when my children have made some mistake, I can remember these examples. In the heat of the moment, when I feel disappointment, fear or anger, I pray my love will be stronger than those emotions. Maybe the next time the principal calls I won't be so anxious. After all, it could be good news.

PRAYER TIME

• SUGGESTED SCRIPTURE: Matthew 6:5-8, 9-15; 18:19-20; 21:22;
Mark 1:35; Romans 8:26-27;
1 Thessalonians 5:16-18; James 5:16;
Psalm 17:6-8; 39:12; 54:2; 55:1; 143:1

Praying as a Family

Families can pray in countless ways, perhaps saying prayers like the Our Father, asking for our needs and the needs of others, singing our gratitude or simply resting in silence in the loving gaze of God. Some families pray the rosary together. Others read and reflect on Scripture. Here are some ideas to help make family prayer time easier:

1. Start simple.

God does not have elaborate expectations for your family. God simply desires your time, attention and openness. It's difficult to remain committed to family prayer that is too long or complicated. Young children, especially, need short prayer. As your children grow older you can encourage them to take more time to pray on their own in addition to the family time.

Find a schedule that works for your family. The best time for prayer is the time that works best for you. For a number of years I drove my children to school every day and that's when we prayed together. Choosing a regular time makes it easier to remember. Praying at bedtime has also worked well for us, although it became more difficult as our teenagers started staying out later. It may be that no time is perfect, and you just do the best you can.

Create a loose structure for prayer. It's helpful if everyone knows about how long the prayer time will be and what it will include. Children are more apt to participate if they know what is expected of them. At the same time, be open to the Spirit and allow freedom within the structure.

2. Be creative.

It's important that children learn traditional prayers, but there's more to prayer than reciting words. Model praying in your own words. Experiment with singing, hand movements or even dance to praise God. Listening in silence is also a crucial part of prayer.

As your family grows and changes, your prayer will change too. What worked last year may not work now. Ask God to show you how and when to pray. There are lots of books and pamphlets on prayer, even Web sites.

3. Set a good example.

Participate fully in your family prayer time. Children will know if you are just going through the motions. Commit to your own private prayer practice as well. Our personal prayer lives feed our family and community. We need face-to-face time with God to strengthen and deepen our faith.

In the years I had young children at home all day, my personal prayer time was hit, miss and sometimes on long sabbatical. But the care of young children, the sick or the elderly can itself be a form of contemplative prayer if approached with love and a spirit of being in the presence of God.

One mother told me, "Some days I lie on the floor in exhaustion next to my little ones and just say 'Jesus' over and over."

Don't be hard on yourself if you miss a day of prayer or get out of the habit entirely. It's never too late to start again. God's not keeping score.

Prayer in Times of Crisis

A woman stood with her middle-aged children near the hospital bed where her husband lay dying. Her son and daughter said their good-byes and hugged their father for the last time. Then she kissed her husband and waited, holding his hand, watching his chest rise and fall.

As he breathed his last, she automatically made the Sign of the Cross, and she and her children began praying, "Bless us, O Lord, and these thy gifts...."

A strange prayer, it seemed, for such an occasion. Though each of them prayed in their own life and attended Mass regularly, this prayer before meals was the only family prayer practice they had shared over the years. It is what they had to fall back on in times of crisis.

Perhaps what matters most is that we do turn to God. The words or ritual we use may be less important. On September 11, 2001, I realized I wanted my children to have something to hang onto in times of crisis, something so ingrained they would cling to it without having to think.

That day my husband and I had joined a standing-room-only crowd at Mass. Not until I left the church did I realize how important that action was for me. Gathering with others of faith, acknowledging our dependence on God, tuning in to the gospel and reliving the paschal mystery all served to center me in the midst of the storm. The world still reeled. I still felt bewildered, frightened, sorrowful and confused. But something now anchored me. I wanted more than anything to give my children that anchor, not just now, but always, in whatever difficulty they might face. My reactions would guide my children.

Attending Mass is perhaps the best option but is not always feasible. Some families pray the rosary together in times of crisis. I asked myself, as a family what do we have to fall back on in time of crisis? What came to mind was the simple blessing cup ritual we used for many different occasions.

So we gathered the family that evening. We lit a candle. We each spoke aloud a few of our many blessings and we gave thanks. We talked briefly about the terrorist attacks, asking the children about their feelings and answering their questions. Our ten-year-old daughter had seen television coverage at school that showed people in the Middle East cheering at the destruction of the twin towers. "Why?" she asked with tears in her eyes. I had no easy answer for her. I tried to explain how sometimes we fear people and ideas we don't understand, and how fear can lead to violence.

Even our teenager, who seems to ration his words like rare treasures, spoke up. "I'm afraid we'll respond with violence," he said.

We read Scripture: "So we do not lose heart...because we look not at what can be seen but at what cannot be seen; for what can be seen is temporary, but what cannot be seen is eternal" (2 Corinthians 4:16-18). We shared our thoughts about the meaning of that verse.

"I don't know what it means," said our eight-year-old in a tone of defiance. I invited him onto my lap and tried to explain in terms he could understand. My husband shared his fears, "Yes, even dads can be afraid, but courage is going ahead and living despite fear, trusting in the One who is always faithful."

We each took turns asking God for what we most wanted or needed and ended by singing a hymn and sharing the familiar blessing cup. Afterward I felt peaceful and connected. I trusted the Spirit was present. My children seemed calm and resumed their routines.

I have my own fears for the future. I know I can't be sure that my children will be safe, or even that they will turn to God in times of trouble. What I hope to give them is something to fall back on, a way of being that is so natural it will play itself out in the midst of panic, uncertainty or suffering.

Family Prayer Ritual in Crisis

- SUGGESTED SCRIPTURE: Jeremiah 29:11-14; Habakkuk 3:17-18; Haggai 2:5; Matthew 28:20; 2 Corinthians 4:16-18

You will need:
Fifteen to thirty minutes
Wine glass or special cup
Juice
Bible

1. Gather the family and acknowledge the crisis. Explain that you are coming together to ask God for help and to support one another. Remind people that the night before he died, Jesus gathered his friends for a meal and shared a cup of blessing with them. Begin with a prayer such as:

    We gather in the name of the Father, Son and Holy Spirit. We come as we are, with our anxiety, our neediness and our uncertainty. We know that you are with us, and that your love is greater than any challenge.

2. Read aloud one of the suggested Scripture passages and ask family members what they heard or what the Scripture meant to them.

3. Ask family members to share their feelings about the current crisis. Explain that everyone will listen respectfully to each other, and that it is OK for people to have different feelings. Each person should only share once, and if it seems people have more to say, you can plan to talk more later after the prayer is finished.

4. Pour juice into the wine glass and raise it up saying: *God bless this cup as a sign of your life, which we share.*

5. Have each person pray for his or her needs before taking a sip. Ask the entire family to answer: *We pray to the Lord.*

6. End with the Our Father.

The Examen: An Everyday Prayer

Attributed to Saint Ignatius of Loyola, founder of the Society of Jesus (Jesuits), the Examen is a prayer form growing in popularity among families. Saint Ignatius developed a spirituality centered on imitation of Jesus. He stressed the need for daily prayer and reflection in order to know God's will in our lives. The Examen is one method Saint Ignatius taught his followers as a way to seek and find God in all things and to gain the freedom to let God's will be done on earth.

I offer here a simplified version of Saint Ignatius's Examen. You can do it alone, with a child or together as a family. It requires only a few quiet minutes at the end of the day.

1. Begin with a quiet moment of gratitude for God's goodness to you today.

2. Reflect on your day and choose a time when you felt happy, connected with others or simply aware of God's presence.

3. Also identify a time in your day when things weren't so good—maybe you experienced bad feelings or felt distant from God. Do not judge these moments; simply bring them to mind, and then offer them to God.

4. Ask the Holy Spirit to give you the mind and heart of Christ, to see as Christ sees.

The benefits of the Examen come from making it an everyday discipline over time. This simple and powerful habit will lead to greater awareness of God's loving presence in our lives, as well as to areas where growth is needed. Undertake this exercise with a spirit of hope and discovery, seeking self-awareness before a loving God.

Jennifer began practicing the Examen with her two boys when they were ages four and eight. "I thought it would be forced and I'd have to work hard to make it happen, but it was really easy," she says. "Now if I forget my youngest, Ewan, will say, 'Mom, what's the best part of your day?'"

The Examen has helped give the family a structure for prayer and go beyond saying thanksgiving and intercessory prayers. Jennifer says it's helped her children see the connection between God and all of life. Why does Ewan like it? Now, age six, he says, "Because it's fun."

5

LABOR DAY BACK-TO-SCHOOL
Work as Cocreation

The Book of Ecclesiastes might well have included, "There's a time for vacation and a time for work." The bittersweet line between them is Labor Day. It's the last hurrah of summer before what has traditionally been the beginning of the new school year. It is a good time for families to reflect on the work we do, whether it's academic studies, a career, parenting or a combination of these.

Most of us need to work to support our families, but if we are not deliberate about our attitudes and practices around work, we can drift into unhealthy habits. The American work ethic, often a source of pride and success, can be twisted into an unforgiving taskmaster. Our days are imbued by the message that we need, need, need and need more. And so we work longer hours to buy more of what we think we need or to alleviate fear that we will not have enough. Some of us just want to earn enough money to retire or pay for some activity, like travel, that we like more than working. We may work, not because we find it fulfilling, meaningful or important to the world around us, but for prestige or power. Others may overwork to feel worthwhile or to avoid facing relationships with others, self or God. Less often we find meaning in the work itself, especially menial tasks or manual labor.

The Roman Catholic tradition honors work as a necessary and privileged sharing in God's artistry. Honest work has value whether performed by an adult, child, highly trained professional or manual laborer. In doing even the simplest task, like laundry, we have the opportunity to become cocreators with God. Through our efforts God works on us, molds us and, through us, shapes the world. The Spirit breathes life and creativity through our labors.

Saint Benedict, one of the founders of monasticism, advocated a healthy balance of prayer, work and leisure. He laid out a *Rule* for his monks to follow that assured this. Most of us do not have the rigid discipline of a monastery in our homes, but we can borrow some

Benedictine insight and practice. We can try to schedule time each day for prayer, work and leisure, to live a thoughtful and reflective life, not just a busy and productive life. We can strive for a balance of time and of being, by paying attention to our feelings and to our body, not just to the clock. We can rest when we're tired, seek nourishment when we're hungry, work when we have energy and inspiration and celebrate and grieve in due time.

This section offers prayer, wisdom and family activities for Labor Day, back-to-school time, work and chores and the dilemma of busyness in our lives.

LABOR DAY

• SUGGESTED SCRIPTURE: Ecclesiastes 3:9-13; Matthew 25:14-30

This holiday gives us an opportunity to focus on the holiness of the everyday work we do. As we participate in the civil festivities, let us also take time to meld the temporal with the spiritual.

Americans celebrated the first official Labor Day in New York City in 1882. It began as a day when union workers marched in the streets to call attention to their fight for better pay, safe working conditions and fair treatment. Eventually, it became a national holiday.

Leaders in the Catholic church have been outspoken over the last century about the importance of the rights and dignity of workers, and these goals remain worthy today.

Labor Day Family Blessing

You will need:
    About twenty minutes
    Paper and pencil
    Candle and matches
    Symbols of work done by family members

Sit down with your children and make a list of work done by family members. Include work in the home, yard or another location. Then ask each person to bring an item that repesents one job they do. For instance, Mom or Dad might bring a tool used in their work. A child who takes out the garbage could bring a clean trash bag. A student could bring a dictionary or calculator.

On a table or other flat surface, arrange the symbols of work around the candle. Light the candle to remind the family of the presence of God.

Leader: This is the day the Lord has made.

All: Let us rejoice and be glad.

Leader: We set aside this Labor Day to ask God to bless our work throughout the year.

All: God of All Creation, bless our work.

Reading: 1 Corinthians 12:4-6 and this quotation by Martin Buber:

"It is not the nature of the task but the consecration that is the vital thing."

Reflection: Ask your children what these readings mean. Do these verses say anything about chores around the house? About a career? Share your own experience too.

Blessing Litany

Using the list of work compiled earlier, pray a litany of blessing. Include a variety of jobs, large and small, done by each person in the family.

For example:

Leader: Bless Mom as she goes to the office.

All: God of All Creation, bless our work.

Leader: Bless Dad as he makes breakfast.

All: God of All Creation, bless our work.

Leader: Bless sister as she cleans her room...

Bless brother as he folds laundry...

Closing Prayer: "Glory be to God whose power, working in us, can do infinitely more than we can ask or imagine" (from Ephesians 3:21). Amen.

CHORES

• Suggested Scripture: Galatians 5:13b; Mark 9:35

Getting kids to do chores may be one of the most challenging aspects of parenting. Often it seems easier to do the work ourselves than to try to get our children to do it. If we see work as cocreation with God, then everyday tasks like making beds, picking up toys and washing dishes become important for our children to do. It is in the home that our children first learn to serve others.

Work within our families prepares children for work in the world. When they are responsible for chores in the home, children feel a sense of belonging and competence. A toddler who learns to pick up her toys grows to know, on a deep level, that she is contributing to the household. A teenager who mows the lawn or helps prepare meals grows into an adult who understands how his labor promotes the common good and fosters unity. Children who practice working together at home will bring a spirit of cooperation to the community.

There is no foolproof method for keeping kids on task. The best strategy may be to keep coming up with new tactics. You will probably need a different motivator for each child and for each stage of development. For instance, one of my children responded best to computer restrictions, while limiting social activities inspired another to get things done. Here are just a few tips:

1. Start young. Almost as soon as a toddler can dump out toys, she can pick them up. The sooner children get in the habit, the better.

2. Let young children work along with you on household tasks like folding clothes, dusting, raking leaves and cooking. Try to relax and enjoy the process. At this stage that is more important than the end result.

3. Training is imperative. Demonstrate the task. Allow your child time to learn the skill. With my five-year-old, I realized after much frustration, that I had to help him make his bed for many months before I could expect him to do it alone.

4. Make chores a consistent part of family life. Explain that everyone enjoys privileges in the family, and everyone shares the responsibilities.

5. Examine your own attitudes about work and what they may be communicating to your child.

6. Collect a bag of tricks. Chore charts, schedules, positive rewards and the withholding of privileges can all help keep kids on the job.

7. Be creative. Ask other parents what works for them. Even ask your children for their suggestions.

BACK-TO-SCHOOL SHOPPING: A TEACHABLE MOMENT

• SUGGESTED SCRIPTURE: Galatians 5:13b; Mark 9:35

How I dread the appearance of those back-to-school sales hammering home the message that summer is almost over and I had better start buying now. It's not the sales that make me blue; I love bargains. It's that over the years, the fun has gone out of school shopping.

Endearing moments of buying a kindergartner's backpack have given way to arguments over shirts sliding up and pants riding down. Instead of tossing packets of brightly colored fat markers in the cart, I'm staring in horror at the cost of a graphing calculator. It grows harder and harder to draw the line between what we need and what we want.

American children are targeted by $12 billion worth of advertising and marketing annually. They spend over $166 billion a year and directly influence $250 billion worth of their parents' spending by requesting or demanding things. Kids may begin to believe their self-worth is based on what they buy.

Maybe I dread school shopping because it's so much more than a trip to the store. It's raising kids to see beyond the prevailing culture of materialism.

"Last year I was lucky," says Angela. "My teenage daughter asked me to take her to the thrift store, and she bought all the clothes she needed for less than $20. This year, her tastes have changed. She wants the latest fashions at the mall. She has her own money from baby-sitting, so that's good, but it does bother me to see her starting these kinds of spending habits."

"For me, the problem is shoes," says Lisa. "My boys wear uniforms to school so clothing isn't a big issue. But, boy, do they want expensive shoes. One wants the latest basketball shoes, the other wants skateboard shoes."

I asked parents for advice on back-to-school spending issues. Here are some tips:

1. *Your example as parents will speak the loudest.*
   Teens naturally want to break out and try new ways of living, but in the long run, the way you spend your money will be the strongest influence on their spending habits.

2. *Set limits.*
   Tell your children how much you're willing to spend. If they want something more expensive, they must pay for it themselves.

3. *Help your child decide how to allocate her income between saving, sharing and spending.*
   A long-term goal, like a bike or college, makes saving easier. Children will feel more generous if they choose to whom they'll donate their money. Help them check out charities to make sure they are legitimate. Encourage kids to stick to their budgets by setting aside savings and charitable giving first. What's left is for spending.

4. *Use shopping trips as practical lessons in value.*
   For instance, compare different products and explain how you might pay more for something that is well-made and will last but that you won't spend extra simply for a fad or name brand.

5. *Youngsters may not yet understand that there is always a new style, something "just out."*
   We can't have it all, and it's never too soon to start learning to choose judiciously. Experience is often the best teacher. If a child spends his whole allowance in one day and can't buy anything for a month, he'll probably be more prudent the next time he has money to spend.

6. *Choose entertainment that promotes your values.*
   To help your children escape the pressure to shop and spend, limit television and computer use.

7. Cultivate gratitude in your family.
Everything we have is gift from God: our health, our home, our money, even our pencils and school clothes. Being grateful means more than a daily prayer of thanksgiving. It means stewardship: remaining accountable for the good use of all things given to us, appreciating what we have, sharing, and not taking more than we need.

Thanks for listening. I feel better already. Talking to other parents and thinking ahead about strategy gives me energy and confidence to face back-to-school shopping. *Now where did I put those sale flyers?*

FIRST DAY OF SCHOOL BLESSING

• SUGGESTED SCRIPTURE: Proverbs 16:3; Philippians 4:13

You may choose to bless your children the night before school starts, perhaps blessing new school supplies as well. Or you may celebrate a special breakfast or dinner the first day of class. Here are some sample prayers and appropriate Scripture readings. There are a number of ways to bless your child. You may place a hand on her head while praying the blessing, or make the Sign of the Cross with a finger on his forehead, or make the Sign of the Cross in the air over your child. You may also bless your child with holy water or oil. Small vials of oil scented with frankincense or myrrh are sold at Catholic supply stores. Explain to your child the oil is not magic, but rather a physical sign of something we cannot feel or see—God's grace.

Prayer for Younger Children

God, bless (name) as she starts kindergarten. Keep her safe in your loving care. Help her to have fun, enjoy learning and make new friends. Amen.

Prayer for Older Children

O God, Giver of all knowledge, bless (name) as he begins school this year. Help him grow in wisdom as well as knowledge and to be kind and conscientious.

God, bless all teachers and students, especially those at (name) school. May their hard work help bring about a better world for us all.

God, we thank you for the opportunity to go to school and for the ability to learn. We ask your blessing on those children who do not have the privileges we enjoy. Keep us mindful of your love today and always. Amen.

GET RHYTHM!

The beginning of the school year marks many milestones of family life. One friend just sent her oldest to off college; another walked hers to kindergarten. These times make us acutely aware of the rhythms of life.

In past generations people's lives more closely followed the rhythms of nature. In autumn people bustled about preparing for winter. They harvested and preserved food, gathered fuel, filled the cracks and patched the roof. Winter came and life slowed; people rested, reflected and rejuvenated. With spring began the work of preparing soil, planting seeds and pruning away unnecessary deadwood. In summer, people tended what had been sown. The season included long days of hard work, but also days of celebration with family or friends.

For many of us, these seasonal rhythms have been replaced. Perhaps by the sports seasons of football and soccer, basketball and volleyball, baseball and more soccer. Or by the consumer buying seasons: back-to-school sales, Halloween candy, costumes and decorations, followed by Thanksgiving, then Christmas shopping, after-Christmas sales, Valentine's Day, Easter and Fourth of July. For the outdoor recreation crowd, it's hiking in the fall, skiing in the winter, cycling and river-rafting in the spring, camping and water sports all summer.

Yet, these new cadences of life offer little or no down time. It's all go, go, go.

I started the summer with hopes of spending carefree hours with my children. I planned fewer commitments, and relished the idea of no schedule. But by August, I couldn't wait for school to start because I needed a break from all the summer activities that had taken over.

As I sit here enjoying in the quiet of my empty house on the first day of school, I fear within a month I'll be stressed again. Will I soon be running between volunteer commitments, prayer group, school meetings, music lessons and sports practices? Will I get yet again caught up in the holiday wind-up this winter and be exhausted when Christmas arrives?

I feel tired just thinking about it. How does one get off this merry-go-round? Just jump off? Is it possible to slow down a bit and then step off? Sometimes I'm tempted to just hold on tight as it goes faster and faster.

Rhythm is such an essential part of nature, it must be important in our lives. How can we be more intentional about establishing rhythm in our days?

One possibility is the Liturgy of the Hours, or Divine Office, which has existed from the earliest centuries of the church as daily prayer for priests and religious. It provides prayers, psalms and meditation for nearly every hour of every day. A simplified version includes Morning Prayer, Evening Prayer and Night Prayer, and the Office of Readings, which can be said any time of day.

This may not seem at all practical for you or your family. But perhaps it offers a structure to strengthen healthy spiritual rhythm in our lives.

Start small. Maybe night or morning prayer is already a habit; add two minutes at noon or before dinner. No need to go out and buy the four-volume set of the Liturgy of the Hours. Use the family Bible to read a psalm or chapter from the Gospels. Hum your favorite hymn while praying the words in your mind and heart. Or sit quietly for five minutes concentrating on the rhythm of your own breathing.

Those experienced with the Divine Office say it works best to decide on the specific times you'll pray each day, and try to stick with that schedule. As you get in the rhythm, you may find you want to increase the amount of prayer, or the number of times. Beware of an overzealous agenda that may set you up for failure.

Establishing a regular pattern of prayer fertilizes the soil so other life-giving rhythms take root.

BEWARE OF BUSYNESS

- SUGGESTED SCRIPTURE: Psalm 5:2-3; 23; Matthew 6:25-29; 11:28-29; Mark 6:31

Listening to conversations at a coffee shop, you'd think it's a badge of achievement to describe one's jam-packed days and busy evenings. Parents have work, volunteer commitments, church activities and exercise routines. Children have homework, sports, music lessons and sleepovers. There is little time to stop and reflect, to realize the rush and pressure are bleeding life from us.

Thomas Merton called the busyness "...a pervasive form of contemporary violence."[3] For many families it is an unquestioned way of life, so much a part of our culture we think it's normal and good. And yet, this busyness may be killing our souls.

A voice of wisdom is rising, whispering in the cacophony of our culture. Like the voice crying out in the wilderness, it urges us to slow down, be quiet, and listen.

"I cleared my calendar. I used to cram as much into a day as possible. But now I have backed out of anything that takes me away from my home during the evening or the weekend," says Laurie, a wife and mother of three. "I stopped going to Parent Club meetings, Safety Committee meetings, Tupperware and Pampered Chef parties."

Laurie and her husband took their children away for an overnight family retreat. They rested, relaxed and took an in-depth look at their time and how they spent it. They came back with a framework that helped them make choices and prioritize.

Bottom line? "You have to know how to say 'No,'" says Laurie. "It's hard, but you can do it because you know you're doing the right thing."

They realized they had a full life just taking care of necessities, like homework, chores, grocery shopping and dental appointments. Looking at the free time left, they decided as a family how to spend it before making outside commitments. The children cut back on sports. They all reduced social commitments. Sunday is set aside for church, family dinner, rest and play.

---

[3] Thomas Merton as quoted in Muller, Wayne. *Sabbath: Restoring the Sacred Rhythm of Rest* (NY: Bantam, 1999), p. 3.

"At first it was really hard because we were in the routine of go, go, go," says Laurie. "But now we're more rested. The house is better kept up. There's less fighting, and more laughter. It's brought into focus what is really important and meaningful in life."

This family's impetus for change was the book *Sabbath: Restoring the Sacred Rhythm of Rest* by Wayne Muller. Muller states the busyness of modern life makes war on our bodies and spirits, our children and communities. Our fast pace disconnects us from the wisdom that grows from rest and reflection. Without regular doses of this wisdom we forget how to love, forget our natural wonder and sensual delight.

Our faith, he says, shows a better way:

> Jesus, for whom anything was possible, did not offer "seven secret coping strategies" to get work done faster, or "nine spiritual stress management techniques'" to enhance our effectiveness. Instead he offered the simple practice of rest as a natural, nourishing and essential companion to our work. Learn from me, he invited, and you will find rest for your souls.[4]

We may not be able to go away to the hills or in a fishing boat to take a break as Jesus did, or even to a hotel for a retreat like the family mentioned above. But we can look for times of stillness in our daily life.

David and Patty and their three children try to make space for quiet with a weekly "no technology day." They don't ban essentials like electricity or the car, but there's no TV or computer.

A father of four stopped working overtime on Saturdays. Another family moved to eliminate the mother's long commute. Returning to work when my youngest child started school, I chose freelance jobs at home rather than resume my stressful career in television news.

If you're living on the run, it is difficult to make changes and slow down. It helps to find a group of like-minded friends. Support each other and share ideas. My friends are often the gauge that helps me see busyness creeping in and the pace speeding up.

It's no new discovery that doing too much can destroy what's most precious in our families. In ancient Chinese the word "busy" is written by combining the character for "killing" with the character for "heart."

---

[4] Muller, p. 24.

Prayer for Parent Feeling Overwhelmed

O God, whose yoke is easy, and burden light, I feel overwhelmed. There is so much to do and not enough time, and I'm tired. There are small details to take care of and big projects waiting for me. I'm pulled in so many different directions all at once. Being a parent is a huge job, and today I'm not sure I can do it. Help me to trust in you. Draw me into the peace of your love. Send your spirit of wisdom to help me take one task at a time, and to decide what is essential and what I can let go. I realize I can't be all things to my children. Help me not to expect too much of myself. Take my efforts and bring them to perfection through your grace. Amen.

KEEPING THE SABBATH

• SUGGESTED SCRIPTURE: Exodus 33:12-14; Deuteronomy 5:12-15; Proverbs 23:4-5; Ecclesiastes 4:6

In Genesis we read that God created the universe in six days and on the seventh day rested from that work. The Sabbath commemorates this event, and illustrates important aspects of God's covenant with the Israelites. The commandment to keep holy the Sabbath is fully one-third of the length of the Ten Commandments. It was to be observed by all, including the alien, the slave and the oxen. It extends from Friday's sundown to Saturday's sundown.

Christians inaugurated a new Sabbath on Sunday to celebrate Christ's Resurrection and establish a new covenant. But Jewish Sabbath tradition and practice remain part of our faith history and offer a beautiful and valuable experience for Christian families. We can adapt Sabbath customs to help keep balance in our lives and focus on God.

For the Jewish people, observing the Sabbath involves far more than refraining from work and going to temple. It means resting in a way that opens space for remembering God's generous and loving creation. It is cultivating an attitude of wonder, and rejoicing that all of life is a blessing. Without the stresses and routine of daily life we have room to hear the voice of God more clearly. Sabbath includes comfort and pleasure, prayer and Bible reading, story and worship, friendship and love. Married couples are encouraged to re-consummate their marriages on the Sabbath.

Jewish Sabbath begins at home when the mother of the family lights the Sabbath candles at sundown. Traditionally, the father recites the Kiddush (prayer of blessing over the wine), lays hands on the children and blesses them and reads a Bible passage. The table is covered with a white tablecloth, and special bread and wine are blessed and served, along with choice food. Special songs add to the celebratory spirit. The day of rest, gratitude and rejoicing lasts until sundown the next day when it is concluded with a farewell ceremony.

In some observant Jewish homes, guests and family are greeted with a Sabbath box when arriving for the Sabbath meal. They place things in the box they will not be using until the Sabbath is over such as car keys, cell phones, wallets and appointment books. This is one habit we can borrow to help remind our families of the need to set aside Sabbath time.

Past generations found it easier to take Sunday off because the culture supported it. Most stores and businesses were closed that day. Today some parents find they must work weekends. Others who work during the week need much of the weekend to catch up on tasks like grocery shopping and laundry. Children playing sports are sometimes cut from the team if they miss Sunday games.

If you can't take Sunday off, try to set aside half a day on the weekend to observe the Sabbath. If this is impossible, try one evening during the week. If all you can manage is one hour squeezed somewhere into your schedule, then start with that. Keeping the Sabbath is a powerful spiritual practice. As the Jewish people sing: In exile, it was not Israel that kept the Sabbath; it was the Sabbath that kept Israel.

Family Sabbath Box

You will need:
   About thirty minutes
   One large shoe box
   Sheet of paper large enough to cover the outside of the box
   Crayons or markers
   Glue

1. Spread the paper on a table or the floor, so that each person has a space to draw or color. Explain that you are decorating a special box that will help the family set aside special time for relaxing together.

While you work, talk more about the idea of Sabbath and about what time would work best for your family to observe it. When everyone has finished their artwork, wrap the paper around the box and glue it into place.

2. Choose a place for your Sabbath box, perhaps on top the refrigerator or in the coat closet.

3. Discuss with the children what items people can put in the box to help them leave aside daily activities and focus on family time, prayer and rest. Items might include the TV remote, computer mouse, car keys, telephone, day planner, checkbook, newspaper and other items symbolic of house and yard work, homework, sports practice or whatever your weekday activities include.

You'll find it easier to be faithful to Sabbath time if you schedule it the same time every week. At first it may feel awkward, even uncomfortable. If you're not used to taking time off to do nothing, you may feel nervous or anxious. Don't give up. Some ideas to try: Take a walk. Read aloud to the family. Take a nap. Tell stories. Visit a park.

6

AUTUMN EMBER DAYS
Remembrance and Thanksgiving

Though our culture has become highly technological, we cannot escape our dependence on and connection with the natural world. As Christians our posture toward these ties is one of deep reverence, awe and gratitude. God created us within an infinite and indescribable tapestry of energy, beauty and mystery.

Since ancient times, we have unraveled many mysteries of nature. We now understand why in autumn the days shorten and the sun stays low on the horizon, events which struck fear in the hearts of our long-ago kinfolk. But many questions remain for which we struggle in vain to find answers. Perhaps that is why celebrations of Halloween, All Saints' and All Souls' Days, with their roots reaching back to ancient times, continue to strike a profound chord in our hearts today.

As winter nears, animals hibernate, trees lose their leaves and plants wither and die. We, too, prepare for the dark to come and acknowledge the thin veil between this life and the next. We remember our loved ones who have died and celebrate our bond with them. For seasons of mourning do come in our lives, seasons of suffering and of death. Confronted with these mysteries, we gather to comfort and remind each other of God's promises. We learn to trust that in dormancy the life force prepares for rebirth.

And so, as generations before us, we give thanks for the fruits of the past year. We gather. We offer hospitality. We feast. We share stories and prayer. This time of remembrance and thanksgiving can be of deep comfort and sustaining joy for our families.

I've adopted the term "Ember Days" for this time of year because of its tradition of fasting, prayer and thanksgiving tied to the harvest season. The word ember stems from Latin and Anglo-Saxon words meaning to *go around in a circle*, as do the seasons of the year. Early Christians adapted the Roman custom of periodic festivals to honor gods and goddesses at harvest and sowing times. They designated one Sunday of each of the seasons of the year a day of thanksgiving for the fruit of that season, be it grain, grape or olive. Eventually days of fasting and prayer began to precede these celebrations of thanksgiving and they were officially established by the church as Ember Days in the eleventh century.

Most of us no longer live lifestyles based on agriculture, but we still depend on the fruits of the earth and those who grow them. So, too, we depend on those who have gone before us and nurtured faith and passed it to us. This section leads us to think, act and pray about our connections with the earth and with the spirit world, or the communion of saints. I've included ideas for celebrating the Feast of Saint Francis of Assisi, Halloween, All Saints' and All Souls' Days, Veterans' Day and Thanksgiving. I've also offered ideas like family storytelling, ritual and prayer to strengthen bonds and offer comfort and courage during times of sorrow and loss.

FEAST OF SAINT FRANCIS: OCTOBER 4

• SUGGESTED SCRIPTURE: Psalm 36:5-9; 104; Matthew 5:1-12

Saint Francis of Assisi is one of the world's most well-known and beloved saints. His life offers something of interest to people of all ages. Young children can understand and relate to his love for animals. Saint Francis' flamboyant youth and rebellion against his parents and social class appeals to many teenagers. His spiritual quest and ever-deepening love for God and others holds inspiration for all of us on the journey of faith.

Francis was born the son of a wealthy merchant in the town of Assisi, Italy, in 1181. A charming young man, he enjoyed fine clothes, good food and drink and fun parties. As a child he had loved the tales of King Arthur and longed for a noble adventure. So when war broke out, Francis became a knight and joined the fighting. He was soon captured, and a year as prisoner of war left him seriously ill. During a long convalescence, Francis began to seek deeper meaning in his life.

His former interests left him empty, and he took comfort in hours of prayer. Inspired by the words of Matthew's Gospel commanding Jesus' disciples to give up their worldly possessions, Francis began to live in radical poverty. His family and friends did not understand. When he refused to stop giving away his father's merchandise to the poor, his father disowned him.

Penniless, Francis begged for food each day while preaching and serving the poor and outcast, such as lepers. He didn't "give up" his comfortable life, as we sometimes give up sweets for Lent. Rather, Francis' experience of Jesus was so compelling that nothing else mattered. He lost his attachment to fine food, nice clothes and comfortable accommodations, wanting only to spend time in prayer and helping others. His example soon attracted many and he formed a band of traveling preachers called the Friars Minor. Within ten years a vast Franciscan movement was sweeping Europe, and his followers numbered more than five thousand.

Francis' all-consuming love for Christ included an understanding of the unity of all creation. He voiced his reverence by addressing all things in nature as Brother or Sister. Creation was sacrament for him. Some of his most intense encounters with God were in a cave or on top of Mount La Verna where he received the stigmata. But his faith was most evident through his loving action. He lived in simplicity and service, depending on God and the generosity of others. Though his life as a single man and leader of the Franciscans is quite different from family life, we can learn from his example and try to emulate his qualities of simplicity of life, reverence for nature, passion for Christ and love and service for the poor and marginalized.

Here are some ideas for celebrating the Feast of Saint Francis:

1. *Learn more through these books and movies about Saint Francis:*
   Francis: The Poor Man of Assisi by Tomie De Paola (Holiday
      House, 1982)
   Brother Sun, Sister Moon: The Life and Stories of Saint Francis by
      Margaret Mayo (Little Brown, 2000)
   The Wolf of Gubbio by Michael Bedard (Fitzhenry and Whiteside,
      2001)
   Franco Zeffirelli's *Brother Son, Sister Moon* (Paramount Studio,
      1972)
   Michael Curtiz's *Francis of Assisi* (Fox Home Entertainment, 1961)
   Animated cartoon, *Francis: The Knight of Assisi* (Ccc of America,
      1997)

2. Practice simplicity with a Giveaway Day.
Have each member of the family take inventory and choose one or
more possessions they do not need. Donate items to charity.

*3. Francis challenges us to bring into our family people who are alone,
poor or somehow isolated from life.*
We don't have to add another commitment to the nursing home or
shelter although these are good, too. All we need do is include people who are left out in what we are already doing. This adds a bit of
simplicity to life.

4. Bless the family pet.
Some churches hold services on the Feast of Saint Francis where
people can bring their animals to be blessed or you can bless your
pet at home. Here's a prayer for the occasion.

> Blessed are you, God of All Creation. We praise you with grateful
> hearts, for you brought forth birds of the air, fish in the sea and
> animals on land. Help us to care for the earth and all living things
> as Saint Francis did. We ask you to bless our pet (name). May
> he/she be a daily reminder of your love for us and your
> marvelous works. Amen.

5. Commit to environmental action.
Choose to do at least one thing that demonstrates your reverence
and care for the earth. Can you decrease trips in the car by combining errands, carpooling or taking the bus? Consider buying
organic or locally grown produce. Can you reduce your household
waste by recycling or buying products with less packaging? Inspect
labels on cleaning products and try to use only those made from
natural and biodegradable ingredients. Read up on land use issues
in your area and contribute your ideas by e-mailing your elected
officials. Make an effort to talk about environmental issues with the
whole family and involve your children in the decision.

Saint Francis is often known as the gentle saint who loved animals. The impact of his life, however, went far beyond this simple
truth. Through a life of service, poverty and love, Francis of Assisi
sparked renewal in the Christian church of his time.

HALLOWEEN, ALL SAINTS' DAY AND ALL SOULS' DAY

From the earliest times of history, the darkening days of autumn have been an occasion to remember and honor the dead. The ancient Celts believed the boundary between the living and the spirit world to be but a thin veil, with one blurring into the other. On the night of October 31, their New Year's Eve, the spirits could walk between the two. The living celebrated into the night by the light of bonfires, feasting and making music. They had nothing to fear if they were reconciled with family and friends who had died. The church often adopted pagan festivals and turned them into Christian holy days. The Celts New Year's Eve is the forerunner of our modern Halloween, the name of which is a contraction of *Hallowmas Eve*, an old name for the night before All Saints' Day.

In the earliest days of the church, Christians remembered the dead at Easter time. Then in the ninth century the church in Western Europe began to commemorate the faithful departed in the fall, when ancient cultures had honored the dead and when it seems the earth itself is dying. All Saints Day was set on November 1 to remember those in heaven and All Souls' Day, November 2 to remember those in purgatory. The Feast of All Saints' is a holy day when Catholics are expected to assemble for Mass.

The Tale of the Jack-O-Lantern

Long, long ago in the land we now call Ireland, there lived a mean and tricky man named Jack. In fact, he was so sly he actually fooled the devil. One night, maybe it was Halloween night, he convinced the devil to climb a tree. As the devil moved from branch to branch, higher and higher, Jack carved a cross in the trunk. The power of the cross is so strong that the devil was trapped and couldn't get down.

To this day, we don't know for sure how the devil got free. But when Jack died, he couldn't get into heaven because he had lived a mean and selfish life. Neither could he get into hell because he had tricked the devil. He was forced to wander the earth until judgment day. He owned nothing but a single turnip, and the devil gave him an ember, which he placed inside the hollowed-out turnip to serve as a lantern to light his way.

As time went by people remembered how Jack had trapped the devil and they began to carry lighted turnips on Halloween to frighten away evil spirits. When Irish families immigrated to the United States, they brought the jack-o-lantern custom with them. Here they began to use pumpkins instead of turnips because they were easier to carve.

Jack-O-Lantern Blessing

You will need:
  About one hour
  A pumpkin
  Knife for carving
  Small candle

Pumpkin carving can be a fun event that includes the whole family. The smallest child can help pull out the pulp and seeds. Preschoolers can help decide whether the face should be smiling or scary. Older children and parents can do the carving. You may want to tell the tale of the jack-o-lantern while you work. When it's finished, gather everyone for a short blessing and light the candle.

Leader: May this jack-o-lantern be a sign that we ask God's help in driving away all evil spirits of selfishness, anger, jealousy and pride.

All: Bless us, O God.

Leader: May this jack-o-lantern be a sign that as a family we all work together for good.

All: Bless us, O God.

Leader: May this jack-o-lantern be a sign of our gratitude for all the gifts of the earth.

All: Bless us, O God.

Light candle.

Leader: May this flame be a sign of Christ's light in the world, more powerful than any darkness.

All: Amen.

Trick-or-Treating

The American practice of trick-or-treating on Halloween probably stems from a custom of ninth century Europe called "souling." During All Souls' Day parades and festivities, poor folk would walk among the homes of wealthier people begging for soul cakes, which were square pieces of bread with currants. In return for the bread, they would promise to pray for the souls of their benefactors' dead relatives.

You might pick one of the following suggestions for adding a spiritual element to your children's practice of trick-or-treating.

1. *To lessen stress, plan a quick, easy dinner.*
   A filling and nutritious menu such as minestrone soup and whole-grain bread will help minimize the effects of any overindulgence in candy later in the evening. Take an extra moment as you say grace to thank God for the generosity of all those who will give treats to the children this evening. Or, in the spirit of ancient tradition, offer a prayer for the souls of those who have died.

2. *Once the costumes are on and everyone is ready for trick-or-treating, pause and lay your hands on each child in turn and bless them.*
   You might say: God, bless this child and keep her safe. Bless all those who generously give treats tonight. Amen.

3. *While trick-or-treating remember to say "Thank you" at each house.*
   Perhaps murmur a simple prayer like "God bless you" before moving on to the next porch.

4. *When trick-or-treating is over and parents have sorted through the treats to make sure they are all safe to eat, gather and ask God to bless the candy.*
   You might pray: Thank you, God, for these treats. May they be a reminder of all the gifts we have received, and may they inspire us to be grateful and generous. Amen.

ALL SOULS' DAY

• SUGGESTED SCRIPTURE: Matthew 5:4; John 1:4-5; Psalm 90:1-2

Family Remembrance Celebration

The following ritual can be celebrated on All Saints' Day, All Souls' Day or any day in early November that is convenient for your family. If you have recently lost someone close to you, your feelings may be too raw and painful for this ritual. Having a time and space to talk about death can be a comfort and a help in working through grief, but people grieve in varied ways, and it is important to be sensitive and accepting of people's differences.

You'll need:
> At least one hour
> Pictures of loved ones who have died
> Several flat sheets of beeswax and wicks for making candles (these can be purchased at most craft supply stores)
> Music and words or a CD/tape for singing "When the Saints Go Marching In" or "The Litany of the Saints"

1. Start the celebration by gathering the family together with a short prayer.

2. Spend some time looking at the pictures of your loved ones who have died and remembering good times you shared with them. Have a box of tissues handy, and be accepting of any sadness and tears that might come up. Mention good qualities you remember in those who have died, and think about how their spirit lives on when you emulate their goodness.

3. The next step is to make the beeswax candles. Demonstrate to the children, beginning by laying one sheet of wax flat on the table, short side facing you.

4. Cut a piece of wick one inch longer than the length of the short side of the wax. Lay the wick at the edge of the wax nearest you. About half an inch of wick should hang free at each end of the wax.

5. Gently, but tightly, fold the wax over the wick and begin to roll up the wax around the wick. Continue until you have rolled up the entire sheet into a candle.

6. You may choose to make a candle for each deceased person, or simply have each family member make one candle. Choose a space, perhaps an end table, mantle, buffet or countertop, where you can leave the candles and photos set up for the month of November. Create an altar by laying out a placemat or small table linen. Stand the candles on saucers or in candleholders and display the photos next to them.

7. Light the candles, dim the lights, and spend a few moments in prayer, perhaps reading a Scripture passage.

Catholics believe that, upon death, souls that are not perfectly free from sin do not go to heaven, but instead spend time in purgatory. Our prayers can speed these souls on their way to heaven. This is a good time to play or sing the "Litany of the Saints" or "When the Saints Go Marching In." Add the names of your loved ones as you sing.

Now turn up the lights, put on some up-beat music and enjoy a simple meal or desert together.

Optional:
Several times we have invited another family or two, or single people to share in this All Souls' Day celebration with us. It works well to give each family their own space and privacy to share their memories and make their candles—perhaps one in the kitchen, one in the dining room and one in the family room. Usually about half an hour is enough time for this. Then gather all the families in a circle to share photos, names and perhaps brief memories of your loved ones who have died. End with a Scripture reading, prayer and song. Then enjoy a meal or dessert together.

Space to Grieve

My first experience with an All Souls' Day ritual came at a family retreat when my children were grade school age. Before arriving I had followed directions on the retreat information sheet and dug through old boxes to find photos of family members who had died. Now with my husband and children gathered around a chipped cafeteria table, I pointed to the faces of my grandparents, captured rather stoically, in the photo from their fiftieth wedding anniversary.

"My grandma had a huge garden," I told them. "I loved to eat her raspberries, gooseberries and peas fresh from the shells. She grew dahlias in a dozen shapes and colors, some the size of dinner plates. We'd walk through the rows and she'd let me choose which ones to snip for a bouquet to take home."

My eyes smarted with tears as I remembered, and I realized with surprise I had never talked about my grandparents to my children. I swallowed the lump in my throat and went on. "What I remember most about Grandpa is the smell of his pipe tobacco. Oh, and how he loved chocolate." It felt so good remembering and telling my children about those happy times.

Then my husband pulled out the photos of his two older half-sisters who had died without ever meeting our children. He had never talked much about them, and now the memories came out in clipped sentences. Anita had been thirteen years older than he, Jeanne eleven years older. They had both died of heart disease. He remembered their funny jokes and playing games with them, and them baby-sitting him. Slowly more detailed memories surfaced and his eyes rimmed with tears as he shared his sadness about his sisters' deaths.

Later, all the families on the retreat gathered in a large circle and held the candles we had made while sharing our memories. Each briefly told about a loved one who had died and we ended in prayer. My husband and I agreed it was a powerful experience of comfort and healing, and we decided to continue the practice each year at home. Our kids enjoyed the candle-making and storytelling. They laughed, telling me I must have inherited my love of chocolate from my grandpa. They had fun picturing their father as a toddler being carried piggyback by an older sister. The feeling of connection was strong between the past and present, between this world and the next. Bonds that cannot be touched or seen began to feel tangible.

In the years that followed, our collection of photos grew and the children began telling their own memories of people who died: a neighbor, a family friend and a woman from the parish. In a few short years, I lost five uncles and a cousin, and we fashioned a special album to hold the photos of our loved ones who had died.

Then came the year death intimately touched our children. For the first time they lost someone they had known and loved all their lives—their grandfather, my husband's father. Our annual All Souls' Day ritual had provided the children an experience of a way in which to grieve. It was familiar and safe to gather and tell stories, to talk openly about the pain and loss of death, and to shed tears without embarrassment.

Once again six months later, on All Souls' Day, we had a time and place to remember how Grandpa loved frozen yogurt, told corny jokes and insisted on good manners. We talked about how much we missed him, we cried and we reminded each other of our hope in the resurrection.

GRIEVING DIVORCE, SEPARATION OR ABSENCE

• Suggested Scripture: Lamentations 3:31-33

Sometimes we lose people, not to death, but through divorce, separation or some other circumstance beyond our control. Perhaps they are not gone forever, but we miss them due to military service or relocation to a distant place. These losses also involve a process of grief and a time of mourning. The candle-making activity above can be adapted to help ritualize and promote healing in these situations as well.

A Psalm in Time of Loss and Grief
(Based on Psalms 6, 22, 40, 57 and Isaiah 40)

Our eyes are dimmed with sorrow;
Our bodies spent with weeping.
Our tongues are numbed to silence
No words to speak our grief.

Comfort us, O God.
Heal us with your compassion.

Draw us into the shelter of your wings;
Hide us in the nest of your love.
Wrap us in the warmth of your healing;
The womb of life and rebirth.

A part of us is missing, ripped away;
This loss has us limping, stumbling blind.
In our hearts, a hole is gaping
Raw, tender, pierced, empty.

Comfort us, O God.
Heal us with your compassion.

Draw us into the shelter of your wings;
Hide us in the nest of your love.
Wrap us in the warmth of your healing;
The womb of life and rebirth.

Comfort us, O God.
Heal us with your compassion.

IN TIME OF ILLNESS

• SUGGESTED SCRIPTURE: Psalm 116; Matthew 8:14-17; Mark 5:25-34;
Romans 8:35-39

Blessing for Healing

Reach out hands in blessing over the sick person, or place a hand on his forehead or shoulder.

Leader: O God, breathe within us the breath of your Spirit as we call out to you.

All: Come, Holy Spirit, with your healing power.

Leader: O God, Giver of life, you made us; we belong to you. Heal our brother/sister (name) in body, mind and soul.

All: Come, Holy Spirit, with your healing power.

Leader: O God, Savior of the world, you love us; we depend upon your forgiveness. Heal our brother/sister (name) in body, mind and soul.

All: Come, Holy Spirit, with your healing power.

Leader: O God, Healer of all, you comfort and re-create us. We long to be one with you. Heal our brother/sister (name) in body, mind and soul.

All: Come, Holy Spirit, with your healing power. Amen.

Prayer for Healing a Sick Child

Place your hand on your child in blessing.

> Dear Jesus, when you walked in Galilee you healed the blind, the deaf and the lame, and you called the little children to come to you. Jesus, we come to you, remembering your promise to hear our prayers. We ask you to heal this child, (name). Amen.

ENCOURAGING FAMILY STORIES

My younger sister, Louise, was born in a snowstorm. Not literally. After driving through blizzard conditions my parents made it to the hospital in time for the birth. But from then on the story was an old standard around my family's kitchen table. We heard again and again how my father shoveled snow to clear the roadway while my mother counted between contractions in the cab of our old truck. My father would usually start the story. We'd have to draw my mother out to hear her side of the tale. My older sister and I would join in, remembering the hot chocolate with marshmallows, a rare treat we enjoyed at the home of family friends where we waited out the ordeal.

Storytelling is the world's oldest entertainment. Even in this age of nonstop opportunity for fun and excitement, nothing captivates us like a good story. And the telling of family tales can be more than just amusement. Stories pass on values, strengthen identity, foster belonging and nurture and explore faith. Family stories can be an important steppingstone for learning to hear the Word of God and live it.

During one recounting of my sister's snowy arrival, a younger brother piped up with his own version of the story. "You weren't even born yet," we told him. "You were dust under the bed."

"I know," he said, "but I was peeking up through the springs."

Like my brother, we all want to play some important part of the action. Telling family stories gives children the chance to experience the power of being part of a living story. When children are well-nourished by stories at home, they are ready to hear Scripture with well-tuned ears. They're ready to see themselves as part of the story of God's people.

Children enjoy many of the stories in Scripture: Noah's ark, Moses and the Pharaoh, David and Goliath—these stories stack up against anything Disney can come up with. But they're no better than the Cartoon Network if we don't see ourselves in them, if they don't come alive for us.

I suggest three things you might try as ways to increase the power of story in your family life.

1. Tape a lined sheet of paper and a pencil on a string to the inside of a kitchen cupboard door. Write down things your children say and do that you want to remember. As the months and years go by, it is fun to read back over these sheets of paper and share memories with your kids.

2. Take ten minutes on Friday or Saturday to read the upcoming Sunday Gospel with your children. Ask questions to draw them into the story such as: Which character do you like most? Which character do you dislike? Or ask them to retell the story from the point of view of one of the characters. For instance, in the Gospel when Jesus chastises his disciples for trying to keep the children away, how might one of the children describe that scene? Maybe you can see yourself in a Gospel story and share this reflection with your children. Are you the hemorrhaging woman in need of Jesus' healing touch? Or a Pharisee, obsessed with rules and regulations, but lacking heart? Be open to both the challenge and comfort of the Gospels.

3. On the drive to Mass talk with your family about the preceding week. How did things go in your family? Did things happen that upset you? Did you like how you behaved? What do you have to celebrate or be thankful for? This may not be the time for an in-depth discussion, simply a calling to mind of our family-week story.

Stories have the power to change us, to affect our lives. My sister was born on a cold and snowy night, but recounting the event created warmth like a glowing fire. The image of my father fighting the elements to bring my mother and the baby to safety lent a security to my childhood world. The images of Scripture can come alive in the same way.

By priming our children to understand stories as ways of reflecting on our experience and opening our hearts to the joys and sorrows of life, we prepare them to hear Scripture as the endless source of wisdom and transformation that it is.

THANKSGIVING

• SUGGESTED SCRIPTURE: Deuteronomy 16:14-15; Psalm 100; Isaiah 25:6-8; Luke 14:13-14

Our American Thanksgiving holiday originated with the pilgrims giving thanks for their survival and a good harvest in a new land. They invited the Native Americans who had helped them stay alive to join in this thanksgiving feast. Similar thanksgiving festivals have been celebrated at harvest time in cultures around the world since people first put down roots and began to depend upon agriculture.

The Jewish Thanksgiving known as Sukkoth, or Feast of the Tabernacles, has been celebrated for three thousand years. Sukkoth takes its name from the small tents Moses and the Israelites lived in during the forty years they wandered in the desert. According to legend Abraham sat in his tent with its flaps open in welcome to all four directions. This symbolized the spirit of generous hospitality evoked by the bounties of nature at harvest time.

Even today in modern times Jewish families often mark the seven-day celebration of Sukkoth by building temporary huts of branches outside in their yards in remembrance of the Israelites' journey and God's faithfulness. They acknowledge that the solid walls and roof of their houses protect them, and at the same time may also isolate them from neighbors, friends and even family members. The first two nights families eat their evening meal outside in the huts they have built. "Dwelling in booths" and exposed to the night sky and the elements they are more conscious of their dependence. They make new once again the spirit of fellowship and generosity that forged their ancestors into a common people as they wandered in the desert so long ago.

The Chinese, Greeks, Romans and Egyptians also held festivals to give thanks for the gifts of nature at harvest. As Christianity grew from a small Jewish sect to the religion of the Roman Empire, authorities adopted these periodic salutes to gods and goddesses of the ancient world. Thanksgiving festivals became days of prayer to the One God and were preceded by days of fasting and works of charity. We can experience the holiday of giving thanks more abundantly by being aware of these ancient underpinnings of the day.

Thanksgiving Table Prayer

O Gracious God, we give you thanks for your overflowing generosity to us. Thank you for the blessings of the food we eat and especially for this feast today. Thank you for our home and family and friends, especially for the presence of those gathered here. Thank you for our health, our work and our play. Please send help to those who are hungry, alone, sick and suffering war and violence. Open our hearts to your love. We ask your blessing through Christ your son. Amen.

Thanksgiving Litany

Leader: We gather to thank you, God, for your gracious care and to ask your blessing.

All: Shout for joy to the Lord. Give thanks to our God.

Leader: Thank you for… (name one thing you for which you are thankful).

All: Shout for joy to the Lord. Give thanks to our God.

Next Person: Thank you for...

All: Shout for joy to the Lord. Give thanks to our God.

(Give everyone a chance to name what they are thankful for, responding to each in turn.)

All: Shout for joy to the Lord. Give thanks to God. Amen.

Thanksgiving All Year Round

"Not crayons and paper, we sent those last year."
"I pick the soccer ball. It comes with its own air pump."
"But how do we know she likes to play soccer?"

"It's the favorite game in her country. All the kids like soccer there."

"What about the inflatable world globe? She could see where we live."

And so went the discussion, our annual tradition of choosing a gift for Maria, the child we sponsor in Honduras. Like Jack Nicholson's character in *About Schmidt,* our family decided to send money each month to help improve living conditions in a poor region of the world. The commitment includes corresponding with a child there.

I wanted to help Maria and her community and share our family's prosperity. I also hoped to give my children perspective, to help them see and be grateful for the abundance in their lives.

It's difficult to know if I've succeeded. My children know Maria lives with only a pit for a toilet. They know her father has abandoned her and that the family lives in a hut with no electricity or running water. Although she goes to school only sporadically, Maria is a skilled seamstress and has sent us samples of her embroidery. My hope is that my children will understand not only Maria's poverty, but her gifts as well. I hope this will give them a lens beyond our cultural context with which to view their own circumstances.

No single practice is likely to insure that our children will grow hearts of gratitude. Like most habits, gratefulness must be continually cultivated. We take time during the Thanksgiving holiday to celebrate and voice that which we hope we are exercising daily throughout the year.

Our faith calls us to ask: How might things look different from the viewpoint of gratitude? My actions might be altered if they stemmed from a mindset of abundance rather than scarcity. Do I see my position, money and power as a mere payoff for my individual effort? I have gained some privileges purely by being born into my time, place and family. Who are the people who have supported my endeavors or paved the way for my success or situation in life?

These questions could spark interesting dinner table discussion for families with teenagers. Parents reflecting on such queries will most likely experience trickle-down benefits in their children. Families with preschoolers will want to start with basic conversations prompting little ones to identify God's gifts in their lives.

Here are a few other ideas to help your children learn the habit of gratitude:

1. *Keep a blessing book.*
Some people use a beautifully bound blank book, but a spiral notebook from the grocery store works fine, too. Each night before bed, family members write down things they are thankful for. As you fill the pages, you'll have a growing record of God's providence in your family life.

2. *Limit TV and trips to the mall.*
Children and adults alike are influenced by commercials designed to create feelings of desire, dissatisfaction and need. It doesn't take national research for me to know that the more time I spend in a store, the more likely I am to find something I "need" to buy. Simply seeing merchandise can make one feel discontent.

3. *Expose children to the wider world.*
Take your children to volunteer at a local food bank or homeless shelter. Invite them, through magazines, movies or TV programs, to learn about the challenges people face in war-torn countries, poverty-stricken neighborhoods and areas of natural disaster. If you can, take your family on a trip to see how people live in other parts of the world. Involve your teens in some experience with the underprivileged. Young adults can spend a week building homes in Mexico or working with children in our own inner-city neighborhoods.

This year think about making Thanksgiving more than just a holiday; make it a way of life.

7

ADVENT AND CHRISTMAS
Waiting in Hope, Living in Joy

• SUGGESTED SCRIPTURE: Isaiah 2:2-5; 10; 11:1-10; 35:1-6, 40:3-5, 9-11;
Matthew 24:42-51; Luke 1:26-38; 1:39-45; 3–8;
Romans 13:11-14; Philippians 1:4-6, 8-11;
James 5:7-10

The season of Advent begins on the fourth Sunday before Christmas. The word *advent* means the arrival of something important. The birth of Jesus was momentously important two thousand years ago and remains so for us today. The time of Advent is set aside for us to prepare ourselves for the great mystery—God becoming human—to unfold once again.

During the four weeks of Advent the Scriptures we hear at Mass are often from the book of Isaiah, which tells the story of the Israelites during their exile in Babylon. God's people had been forced from their homes and taken far from the land they loved. Their cities and villages had been destroyed, and their treasure pillaged. Foreigners in an alien place, they cried out for a savior to deliver them.

We listen to these readings and realize that we, too, experience our own places of exile, our own yearning to return home to the heart of God. Advent gives us time to practice waiting in hopeful expectation, waiting for light to scatter the darkness, waiting for the touch of our savior in our world today.

As Christians we may feel alien in a culture that focuses on the consumer aspects of the season. However, we are also drawn into a whirlwind of shopping, decorating, baking, holiday programs, parties and volunteer efforts to help the needy. While all of these may be good things in and of themselves, they may take over to such an extent that we have little time and energy to devote to our deepest and truest hungers. Advent flies by in a flurry of motion, and when Christmas comes we've missed an opportunity to grow in deeper understanding of the mystery of God being born a babe in a stable.

Staying centered on the spiritual dimensions of Advent and Christmas is a formidable challenge. We can't completely insulate our families, but we can refuse to be taken in by the false glitter of consumerism. We can offer our children what truly fills and delights the heart. No matter how many toys on their wish list, what kids really want, toddler to teenager, is a sense of belonging and security and a feeling of value gained from using their own God-given gifts. This section offers a variety of Advent activities and rituals for families. Don't try to do them all, but feel free to pick and choose according to your family's needs. Start simple and stay focused to enjoy, not the perfect holiday season, but rather a period of time for both waiting and joy. Such an effort helps open our lives to the reality of a God so generous he gave his only Son that we might have life in abundance.

ADVENT WREATH TRADITIONS

The history of the Advent wreath is long and symbolic. And yet it can be a simple ritual easily adapted to different family needs and routines. Advent wreaths can be purchased at most Christian book and supply stores, as can booklets containing prayers, Scripture and reflection for the Sundays of Advent. Or you could make your own wreath and develop your own ritual. The information and blessing below will help you get started.

The traditional Advent wreath is composed of four candles—three purple and one pink—set in a wreath of greenery. The first candle is lit the first Sunday of Advent and an additional candle each remaining Sunday. The pink candle marks the third Sunday of Advent, Gaudete Sunday. *Gaudete* means *rejoice* in Latin, and on this day we celebrate that Advent is half-finished and Christmas is near. The color pink symbolizes joy. The purple of the other candles symbolizes the prayer, penitence and humility with which we prepare for Christmas. Evergreen boughs signify new life, and the circle of the wreath represents the eternity of God's love.

Evidence suggests the roots of the Advent wreath stretch back to pre-Christian Germanic peoples who decorated their homes in the dark of winter with wreathes of candles. Suspended from the ceiling in the main room of the home, they were a mark of hope that the longer, lighter days of spring and summer would soon return. By the 1600s many Catholic and Lutheran families in Eastern Europe had adapted this custom to their Advent celebrations. The lighted candles are a tangible reminder of that for which we wait, Christ, the light of the world.

Family Advent Wreath Lighting

You will need:
    About ten minutes
    Four candles
    Matches or lighter
    Bible

Song or music such as:
    "O Come, O Come Emmanuel" (unknown author)
    "Soon and Very Soon," adapted by William F. Smith (Bud John Songs, Inc.)
    "Stay Awake," lyrics and music by Christopher Walker (OCP Publications)

Sunday dinner is a good time to light the Advent wreath. Some families keep the wreath on their table throughout Advent and light the designated candles each time they gather for a meal.

1. You may want to begin with a brief prayer such as:

> Come, Lord Jesus, be light for our darkness. Send us your Spirit so that we might faithfully spread your love into all the dim and shadowy places of people's lives. Amen.

2. Light the candle.

3. Share a Scripture reading, perhaps one from Sunday Mass or one of these: Psalms 42:2-3; Isaiah 9:2, 6-7; Matthew 3:1-12; Romans 8:19, 22-25.

Some families do best with a quick prayer; light the candle and move on to dinner. Others enjoy a longer ritual. When my children were young they enjoyed a procession to the wreath. We'd turn out most of the lights in the house and one child would carry a lighted candle and lead the others marching from the front door, through the living room to the dining room. We'd sing "O Come, O Come Emmanuel" and finally gather round to light the wreath and read a Scripture passage.

Another way we have celebrated Advent is by placing electric candles in the windows of our home. As with the wreath we started with one on the first Sunday of Advent and added another each week until Christmas.

An Advent Leap of Faith

The day after Halloween my ten-year-old daughter started counting the days until Christmas. I was still digging carrots from my garden and waiting for the leaves to fall from our sycamore tree. I wasn't ready to start thinking about Christmas. Mostly I wasn't ready to tackle all the work that comes with Christmas.

What would it be like, I wondered, if there were no presents to buy, no cards to write, no cookies to bake, no decorating to do? I enjoy each of these activities, but doing them all in the first three weeks of December can be overwhelming. What if all I needed to do to get ready for Christmas was take some extra quiet time each day to prepare my heart for the coming of Jesus? Advent could be quiet and prayerful rather than busy and stressful. I tried to imagine a Christmas with me feeling rested and spiritually rejuvenated with a deeper understanding of what it means that Christ was born a human baby and is ever-coming to life in our world.

Wait before you start yelling "Bah, humbug!" at me. I'm not telling you to throw out the Christmas tree. But I do think we've been sold an empty bill of goods when it comes to the modern American Christmas. It's not only the blatant commercialism that has taken over the true spirit of the holiday; many of us are also caught up in producing a heartwarming storybook family environment. We need to confront these temptations head on.

It's not easy. Like many of you, my husband and I have struggled to keep Christ at the center of Christmas. Years ago when our oldest was four, we decided our family would no longer believe in Santa Claus. I felt like an ogre, or at least a killjoy. How could I rob my children of the innocent fun of all that the myth entails? What could compare to the wide-eyed wonder of a child running to the tree on Christmas morning to see if Santa had come?

I decided to take a leap of faith. I had to believe that the real Christmas story could measure up to "The Night before Christmas." I had to trust the story of a God who loved his creatures so much he gave up all his power and glory to become like them. I had to have faith that the deepest hungers of our hearts would be filled without jolly old Saint Nicholas just opening his pack.

Looking back, perhaps we hedged our bets. We still have presents on Christmas. But we try to emphasize that we give each other gifts as a way of showing our love for one another and as a symbol of God's gifts to us. We've scaled back, trying to reduce our kids' expectations. And we've planned fun family times throughout the season so the excitement doesn't peak on Christmas morning.

I don't want to take the celebration out of Christmas. It is a time for feasting and joy. Decorating, baking and partying with friends and family are all appropriate ways of celebrating Jesus' birth. But I know I can't do it all. If I want to make room for quiet prayer time, simple family fun and sharing with others, some other good, fun things have to go. Each Advent I ask myself, how far am I willing to leap in faith?

TRADITIONS AROUND THE MANGER

Whether it is called a manger scene, crib, Nativity set, or crèche, this is one of Advent and Christmas's most beloved traditions. I highly recommend getting unbreakable Mary, Joseph and Jesus figures so that your children can play with them. Manipulating the characters and acting out the Nativity story was a favorite activity for my young children during Advent. In the early years when we had only a few figurines, miniature Donald Duck and Mickey Mouse filled in for the shepherds. The wise men looked suspiciously like Teenage Mutant Ninja Turtles. Initially, I told the story as the children played, and soon they took over the speaking parts themselves. The story may have varied time to time from the Gospel accounts, but it had become real to the children. So much so, in fact, that I remember once my youngest, who was about three, burst into tears when he was told there was no room at the inn.

The Nativity has been portrayed in art down through the ages, but its popularity as a Christmas tradition began in Italy in 1223 when Saint Francis reenacted what many believe was the first living Nativity scene at the monastery at Greccio. Villagers who came to watch that

Christmas Eve were touched at the sight of a babe in a manger with an ox and donkey standing by. Churches in Italy began to erect Nativity scenes each Christmas, and prominent families soon fashioned their own, sometimes commissioning well-known sculptors to create the figures. The custom soon spread to middle class and poor families as well, through Europe and then the world. In 1953, apparently worried the popularity of the Christmas tree would outshine the manger scene, a small dedicated group called the European Crib Friends formed with the blessing of Pope Pius XII to propagate the tradition.

Bring out the Nativity scene at the beginning of Advent. It is a good way to focus your family on the real meaning of Christmas in the weeks to come. There are many traditions surrounding the crèche, and you can also start your own. Here are a few ideas:

1. *Allow children to play-act the story of Jesus' birth.*
   As mentioned above, this can provide hours of creative fun, and helps children to learn the Christmas story and relate to it.

2. *Say evening prayer before the manger.*
   The novelty of the crib makes prayer time extra special, and children enjoy praying to the Baby Jesus.

3. *Create a soft bed for Jesus.*
   Begin with an empty manger and a supply of straw or shredded paper. Allow the children to add a single piece of bedding to the manger whenever they do a kind deed. Suggest they do their kindness in secret.

4. *Practice waiting.*
   Consider starting with only the figures of Mary and Joseph placed at some distance from the manger. Move them a bit nearer each day of Advent, reflecting on their journey to Bethlehem. Add the remaining figures as the Christmas season progresses with the Wise Men finally arriving on Epiphany, January 6.

Family Blessing of the Nativity

• SUGGESTED SCRIPTURE: Psalm 130:5-8; Luke 1:46-55; 2:1-7;
Mark 13:33-37

You may bless your Nativity scene at the beginning of Advent, on Christmas Eve or anytime in between.

Leader: We begin in the Name of the Father, the Son and the Holy Spirit.

All: Amen.

Leader: God, open our hearts to your Word as we gather to bless our manger scene, a reminder that you sent your son Jesus as our Savior.

Reader: Read from the bible or a storybook.

Leader: Let us raise our hands in blessing over this remembrance of Jesus' humble birth.

Lord our God, with the birth of your Son your glory breaks on the world. Through the night hours of the darkened earth we your people watch for the coming of your promised Son. As we wait, give us a foretaste of the joy that you will grant us when the fullness of his glory has filled the earth, who lives and reigns with you for ever and ever.

THE FEAST OF SAINT NICHOLAS: DECEMBER 6

Celebrating the Feast of Saint Nicholas can help families set a tone for Advent and Christmas that is fun and still focused on the real meaning of the holiday. Saint Nicholas is one of the most popular and well-known saints, and his feast day is observed around the world.

Many legends surround this man who is the original "Santa Claus." He was born about three hundred years after Jesus in the area we now know as Turkey. As a young man Nicholas became a monk and eventually rose to archbishop. The stories we hear are not about a rise to power but about a man who showed a great love for children. They are about a man who practiced charity and compassion for the poor.

One of the most well-known stories of Saint Nicholas tells of a poor man with three daughters. The family was so poor they nearly starved, and so the father feared he would have to send his girls into slavery, thinking that at least then they would have food to eat. Nicholas heard of the man's troubles, and in the dark of night he tossed three bags of gold down the family's chimney.

In Austria, it is believed that God rewarded Nicholas's generosity by allowing him to return to earth each year and bring gifts to children. The children leave shoes outside their doors in hopes the saint will pass by and leave small toys, oranges, nuts or candy. They imagine him dressed in flowing bishop's robes, with a staff and a large book listing their good deeds. Gifts will be left for only those who have been good the previous year.

In other regions, such as Bulgaria and Greece, Saint Nicholas is famous as the protector of sailors and fisherman. Stories tell of him calming the seas and saving ships in danger. A day's catch may be offered to him on his feast day, and children picture the saint with clothes soaked in brine and sea water dripping from his beard. He is celebrated with feasting and parades of decorated boats.

In France, Saint Nicholas is known as the protector of children. A popular story there tells of a wicked butcher who lured three lost boys into his shop. There he salted them away in a tub of brine. Only a miracle could bring a happy ending to this story, and that's exactly what Saint Nicholas is credited with—bringing the boys back to life and restoring them to their families.

In Russia, Saint Nicholas has yet another face. There he is celebrated as the patron of farming and cattle. For six centuries people in the region of Kirov have made a three-day pilgrimage carrying an icon of Saint Nicholas for fifty miles.

Under the Soviet Communist government, only a few people had continued the tradition, but now it is steadily growing more popular again. At one time, six-thousand faithful made the pilgrimage, ending with a Mass of Thanksgiving for the miracles of this long-ago bishop.

Consider celebrating the Feast of Saint Nicholas in your own family. A fitting way to mark the feast day is with an act of generosity toward the poor. First take time to read or tell the story of the real Santa Claus to your children. A list of suggested books is offered on the following page. Then ask your children to think of ways the family might follow the example of Saint Nicholas by helping those who are needy. Pick one thing your family can commit to. Before bed, your children may want to put out a shoe just in case Saint Nicholas visits.

(Have gold foil-covered chocolate coins on hand to leave in their shoes.)

Some ideas for sharing with the needy:

1. *Go shopping for blankets or coats or toiletries and drop them off at your local homeless shelter.*
   If you live in a warm climate, phone and ask the shelter what types of personal items are needed.

2. *Buy a bag of groceries and donate it to the food bank.*

3. *Offer an evening of childcare to a single parent you know.*
   Involve your whole family in preparing a simple dinner and fun games or activities for the children.

4. *Visit a bookstore and let your children pick out their favorite books.*
   Buy them and give them to an agency able to put them in the hands of boys and girls who might not have books of their own at home.

Some books about Saint Nicholas:
> *St. Nicholas: The Wonder Worker* by Anne E. Neuberger (Our Sunday Visitor, 2000)
> *The Real Santa Claus* by Marianna Mayer (Dial, 2001)
> *Saint Nicholas: The Real Story of the Christmas Legend* by Julie Stiegemeyer (Concordia, 2003)
> *Wonderworker: The True Story of How St. Nicholas Became Santa Claus* by Vincent A. Yzermans (ACTA, 2004)

A Night Prayer for the Feast of Saint Nicholas

God, thank you for the loving heart you gave Saint Nicholas. His generosity and kindness is a wonderful example of your love for the little ones, the poor, those tossed about by life's storms. Tonight as Saint Nicholas is remembered around the world, help us to have loving hearts, too. Help us to be strengthened by the stories of his kindness and courage. Through our celebration of this holy man, may we grow to be more like him. Amen.

COUNTERING CHRISTMAS CONSUMERISM

I remember the year Microsoft introduced its new video game console, the $300 X-box just in time for Christmas. Also in the race for our shopping dollars was Nintendo's new system—the $200 Game Cube. Both were competing with Sony's PlayStation and PlayStation2, already gracing 33 million American households.

I felt under attack. With a giant like Microsoft dedicating half a billion dollars to promote its style of Christmas, and what's important in our lives, how could Christian parents compete? And that's only one of the corporations telling our children Christmas comes from a store. Advertising expenditures run around $135 billion each year in America, with more than one-quarter spent between Thanksgiving and Christmas.

To do battle against a force of this magnitude requires definite preplanning and a solid vision of what you want Christmas to be about in your family. If you don't want it to be all about what money can buy, you'll need to start by making time and space for something else.

We begin Advent with a critical look at the calendar, slashing without mercy all but the most necessary commitments. Then each person chooses one fun activity, like a game night with hot chocolate, watching the video of *A Charlie Brown Christmas* or snow sledding. These plans are scheduled along with school programs, decorating the tree and reconciliation service. Everyone must participate with no complaints.

Over the years the children have made unique choices that celebrate their talents or preferences, and even I have learned to show enthusiasm for projects that are not my favorite. We've enjoyed drawing cartoons, a family concert including varying levels of band instruments, a Twister tournament and a drive round town to see Christmas lights. It gives everyone something special to look forward to besides presents. We often schedule the activities in late December to lessen after-Christmas letdown. It's important to beware these don't become simply more things to do in a busy schedule. We do them instead of shopping, making Christmas candy or some other tradition we've chosen to give up.

When you shop, consider looking for ways to spend and still be in solidarity with the majority of humankind who do not have that luxury.

1. Buy environmentally friendly local products that help your neighbors earn a living wage—books from an independent bookstore, hand-crafted furniture, organic produce or pottery at a farmer's market.

2. Support musicians and artists by attending concerts and buying art.

3. Eat at local restaurants and leave a big tip. Instead of giving actual presents to friends or coworkers you would like to thank, give gift certificates for house cleaning, tree pruning, massage or yoga instead.

4. Shop for handcrafts from developing countries sold through organizations which guarantee workers a just wage for their labor and skill.

Industry analysts say video games have preempted low-tech fun like Monopoly and Scrabble. Let's not allow them to take Christmas too. Let's not trade the riches of relationships and the joy of creativity for the empty twinkle and tinsel of the latest contrivance money can buy.

CHRISTMAS TREE TRADITIONS

The Christmas tree is one of the most beloved holiday traditions and has the potential to evoke ancient and powerful symbolism. With its fresh scent, bright lights and beautiful texture and shape, a Christmas tree appeals to our senses as well as taps into our yearnings for hope and the promise of joy.

Is it possible to improve upon the Christmas tree? Probably not. But we can get caught up in meaningless glitz and get so busy we forget to enjoy simple pleasures. Take time to gather the family around the tree this season for prayer, games or stories, and you'll deepen your experience of Christmas.

Some evidence suggests the roots of the Christmas tree stretch back seven thousand years to the ancient Egyptians, who believed evergreens symbolized the triumph of life over death. They marked the winter solstice by bringing green date palm leaves into their homes. Later the Romans also celebrated the shortest day of the year by decorating their houses with greens and candles. Similarly the Druids used evergreen branches in winter solstice rituals and placed boughs over doors to protect against evil spirits.

Martin Luther is known as the father of our modern Christmas tree. According to legend, one Christmas Eve as he walked through the forest he was struck by the beauty of the snow-covered fir trees sparkling in the starlight. Wanting to inspire his family, he chopped one down, brought it home and decorated it with candles.

Eventually the custom spread to the New World, possibly by way of Hessian troops during the American Revolution. It was not universally accepted, however. Puritans in New England banned decorating trees and all other Christmas frivolity. Such attitudes remained in strict Christian circles into the late 1800s, but by the turn of the century one in five American homes had a Christmas tree. This year thirty-five to forty million families in the United States will light up a holiday tree as a matter of course.

Here are some ideas for enriching your family Christmas tree traditions.

1. Before you select your tree check out what Scripture says about trees.
   Hints: Genesis 2:9, Psalms 96:12; Isaiah 11:1; Acts 10:39; Revelation 22:2

2. Consider waiting until Christmas Eve to put up your tree, creating a burst of colorful light to welcome the Christ Child. More than a decoration, the Christmas tree is a powerful symbol of the fullness of Light coming through the birth of Jesus. Lighting the tree each night from Christmas Eve through the Baptism of Jesus in January gives families time to celebrate the end of Advent and waiting, for Christ has come.

3. Ask the children ahead of time to write a short blessing for the tree, perhaps one line each, or you may use the blessing on the following page.

4. Check your library or local bookstore for the picture book *The Three Trees* by Angela Elwell (Cook Communications). This story is appreciated by all ages.

5. Gather round the tree and sing carols or share family stories of Christmases past. Children love to hear about how they acted when they were babies or toddlers.

6. Play "I Spy." One person spies something on the tree and names the color. Others guess until someone gets it right. Make sure everyone gets a chance to spy and to guess.

Family Christmas Tree Blessing

It may be a good idea to plan your blessing the day after you bring the tree indoors and decorate it. Dysfunctional lights, gnarly tree trunks, missing stars and emotional decorators can thwart even the best-laid plans. The best time for the tree blessing is when family members are relaxed and in a positive and prayerful mood.

Begin by standing around the tree and raising a hand in blessing.

God of All Creation,
bless this Christmas tree and us who gather round.
Its beauty awakens in us a memory of paradise,
a promise of eternal life.
God Who So Loved the World,
we wait for your Son, Jesus,
the shoot sprung from the tree of Jesse,
to come to birth in us.
God of trees and stars,
help us to love one another and all the earth. Amen.

Join hands and sing "O Tannenbaum" or another song your family enjoys.

Serve a snack like sliced apples and cheese or graham crackers and hot cider. Choose one of the activities listed above or one your family particularly enjoys.

CHRISTMAS EVE TRADITIONS

• SUGGESTED SCRIPTURE: Matthew 1:18-25; Luke 2:1-20

Many families practice long-standing Christmas Eve traditions, which serve to connect the generations and bring genuine joy and meaning to the holiday. The main challenge when people marry and begin their own families is to combine two sets of experiences and customs in a satisfactory way. Celebrating our first Christmas together, my husband and I discovered a disagreement we had never thought to get straight before the engagement and wedding. My family always put the star on the top of the Christmas tree first and then the remaining lights and ornaments. His family trimmed the entire tree and at the very end crowned it with the star. We can laugh about this now, but at the time it provoked a heated argument. We learned it is important to discover the feelings beneath such disagreements and to deal with them as compassionately as possible.

Holidays like Christmas and other important family events tend to stir up strong feelings, which by nature are often tied to our practices surrounding the day. For this reason it is important to reflect and plan how you'll mark special times like Christmas Eve. You can combine family traditions, or you may want to begin completely new. As your family grows and changes, you may find your celebrations change as well.

Christmas Eve is a good time for blessing your Christmas tree or Nativity scene if you haven't already done so. Some families bake a birthday cake for Jesus and have a birthday party. Every year since their children were toddlers, Therese and John have made a gingerbread birthday cake with a little plastic Jesus on top. After singing "Happy Birthday" and eating cake on Christmas Eve, the youngest child carries the baby Jesus to the empty waiting manger.

As a bedtime story, you can read your children the Christmas Story from the Bible or children's book.

Christmas Eve Prayer

Many parishes now celebrate a children's Mass early on Christmas Eve which is convenient, and geared especially toward youngsters. If you don't attend Mass on Christmas Eve, you may choose to gather your children for a Christmas Eve prayer such as the one below.

> Glory to God in the highest,
> God of the angels; God of the shepherds,
> God of the people; God of the animals.
> Glory to God in the highest,
> You sent Jesus to save us.
>
> On this holy night, you shone light in the darkness—
> The darkness of the skies and the darkness of our hearts.
> On this holy night, Mary gave birth to your love—

Love for a cold and hungry world, love for all the empty places within us.

Glory to God in the highest,
God of hope; God of peace.
God of joy; God of love.
Glory to God in the highest.
Blessed Be God our Savior.

CHRISTMAS MORNING

The Christmas Candle

You will need:
   About five minutes
   One long-burning candle
   Matches or lighter
   Music or words to "Joy to the World," "Hark the Herald Angles Sing" or another Christmas song your family enjoys

1. First thing Christmas morning gather the family around the Christmas tree or the manger scene. Begin with this or a similar prayer.

   O God of All Glory, we are filled with joy this Christmas morning. You so loved the world you sent your son Jesus to be our savior. We light this candle and keep it burning throughout the day as a symbol of how your love lights the world and dispels darkness for all time. May it be a reminder to us to reflect your love in all we do. Amen.

2. Light the candle and join in signing a Christmas carol.

3. Place the candle where it can burn safely throughout the day. Gather before bedtime to extinguish the flame. You might pray the following before blowing out the candle.

   Dear Jesus, we thank you for this celebration of your birth. We thank you for (each person might name one thing they are especially grateful for this day). As we put out the Christmas candle keep us ever mindful that your love never goes out. With your help may we grow each day as your faithful disciples. Amen.

4. Blow out the candle.

HOME FOR THE HOLIDAYS

Over the river and through the woods, to Grandmother's house we go....

The words to this old song conjure images of loving family relationships and cheerful holiday gatherings.

Holidays were less complicated back when "the horse knew the way to carry the sleigh." But family relationships have always been challenging, and Christmas may be the most difficult time of the year for some families.

"It's so stressful taking the kids to Grandma's house for Christmas," says one mother. "My sister has two little girls who come decked out in their velvet dresses and play quietly. I have three rough-and-tumble boys I have to watch every second in order to protect my mother's fragile Christmas decorations."

"The problem for me is video games," says another parent. "We don't have them at home, but that's all my children's cousins seem to play. It makes the whole visit a struggle between me and my kids."

"My family is great," says one dad. "I like being together for the holidays, but they all think I'm a religious nut just because I want to say a blessing before meals. I want to raise my children to know the real meaning of Christmas, but Christ is not central to most of my extended family."

If you find yourself dreading the thought of Christmas with relatives, take heart; a little planning ahead can make a big difference. A picture-perfect holiday may not grow on your family tree, but a few simple strategies can relieve some of the stress and keep you in the Christmas spirit.

Before the holiday arrives take time to reflect. Pinpoint the difficult aspects of your family get-togethers. Decide what you can live with, and what you can't.

Use a calm, non-blaming manner to talk with family members about your needs. For example: Don't say, "Mom, you have all these fragile things around. You're just asking for my boys to break them." Try a less accusing tone, for instance, "Mom, your decorations are lovely. I'm so afraid my boys might accidentally break them. May I please help you move them out of reach?"

Seek understanding rather than agreement. You may never agree with your brother-in-law's atheism, but by listening with genuine interest, you may be able to understand the feelings behind his views and come to accept him as he is.

As the holiday draws near, come up with a game plan to deal with specific crises. For instance, if your relatives like to argue politics, the latest election could turn Christmas dinner into a raging debate. My eleven siblings and I all have strong opinions. Whenever any of us get together there's a chance sparks could fly. My husband and I developed a secret signal we use when things begin to heat up. One of us makes the sign and we escape to meet in private. The bathroom, the back porch or a ten-minute walk will do. We take a breather, give each other a hug and ground ourselves in our love for each other. With this tactic at the ready, we know we'll survive to fight another—oops, I mean celebrate—another holiday.

We've also discovered it helps to think ahead about issues that might develop with our children. Video games, computer and TV have been problems for us. While visiting relatives we adults often get caught up in conversation, the children disappear and at some point we discover they've spent three hours playing video games. We notice this can cause crankiness, fighting and increased insolence in teenagers. We've learned the hard way that proactive is better than reactive. It's easier to enforce limits if the children have agreed to them beforehand. One year we held a family meeting to discuss the upcoming Christmas visit. Our kids drew up a list of alternative activities they'd enjoy doing with their cousins. Since we would be away from home five days and visiting two different families, we also agreed we'd take just ten minutes each day to be alone together and reconnect as a family. This way we can be sure to check in with the kids and resolve problems before they grow unwieldy. We also scheduled in family prayer time.

And I determined to let go and relax my standards a little. After all, Christmas comes but once a year.

CHRISTMAS JOY LIVES ON

Contrary to popular belief, Christmas is not over on December 26, when all the after-Christmas sales begin. Christians continue to celebrate the joyous occasion of our Savior's birth until the Baptism of our Lord, which generally falls on the second Sunday of January. An evenly paced Advent and Christmas season which offers time for quiet reflection amid the joyous celebratory activities will be more life-giving for your family than one that crescendos to a climax on Christmas Day and then ends abruptly. The New Year offers numerous opportunities to celebrate faith and nurture the joy of Christmas in your family.